T0273365

DOUBLETHiNK / DOUBLETALK

DOUBLETHINK*/

NATURALIZING SECOND THOUGHTS

Not innovating wilfulness,
But reverence for the Archetype.
—Herman Melville, "Greek Architecture"

*Adapted from George Orwell's *1984*, quoting Emmanuel Goldstein's *Theory and Practice of Oligarchical Collectivism*: *Doublethink* is "the power of holding two contradictory beliefs in one's mind simultaneously."

DOUBLETALK†

AND TWOFOLD SPEECH

EVA BRANN

PAUL DRY BOOKS
Philadelphia 2016

† Translation of *Dissoi Logoi*, the Pythagorean-Sophistic double account of soul and world; also of *Antilogiai*, "antinomies, antitheses, oppositions."

First Paul Dry Books Edition, 2016

Paul Dry Books, Inc.
Philadelphia, Pennsylvania
www.pauldrybooks.com

Copyright © 2016 Eva Brann
Printed in the United States of America

ISBN 978-1-58988-113-6

To my country and my school,
America and St. John's College

CONTENTS

PROLOGUE

To the Kind Reader,

Here's how I went about making the Table of Contents, literally: I measured my kitchen table and subdivided it into cells 8½" × 5½", a standard half-sheet, usually accommodating one aphorism. The number of cells turned out to be forty, and that's the number of catch-all headings I thought up. (Thus "Death" includes "Old Age," which isn't quite the same.) Under these I distributed my one thousand and some thought-bits. The more I looked at my forty, the less they fit themselves into a *catalogue raisonné*; indeed, any ordering just seemed to twist askew the synapses between thought-cells.* So I left well enough alone and reverted to the ultimate non-sense listing, the alphabet, which is all convenient convention and doesn't impose a smidgen of sense. Thus, although the random arrangement evinces a lot of serendipity, it imposes no order,

> Nor need you mind the serial ordeal,
> Of being watched from forty cellar holes
> As if by eye pairs out of forty firkins.†

Yet I have a conviction, sometimes deep and again merely hopeful, that the result is a whole rather than a

1

heap. Nonetheless, I'd be glad to hear that people picked around and culled what spoke to them. There is, after all, a lot, too much. And ΜΗΔΕΝ ΑΓΑΝ, "Nothing Too Much" said the front hall of Apollo's temple at Delphi to the suppliant coming for his oracle.‡ Just so—but then again, let the warning reflect on itself: In matters that matter, moderate your moderation. Sometimes there is no Too Much.

There was an earlier collection of mine about which several readers told me that they kept it on their bed-side table, clearly meaning it as a compliment. I had my doubts. But once you buy my book or have it on loan, it's yours (the content, that is; the borrowed object you have to give back). So if it serves as a relaxant—well, I meant it a little bit the opposite, but let it be.

And, oh, an explanation of the title *Doublethink/Doubletalk*.§ By doublethink I mean a way, *not* a method, technique, process, protocol, or program, but a spontaneous readiness to do mental double-takes: A position emerges and right away arises its antithetical complement. Thus the account of the way things are that I give to myself tends—not a hand-waving "just happens" but a trustful "expects"—to develop a double vision, a second sighting. Sometimes it is a reaching glance thrown beyond the edges into the infinite territory of the delimiting, and so defining, negation of a position; sometimes it is a translucent tinting by the superposition of another domain; sometimes it is a simple sense of a potent alternative, or a sudden surrender to the claims of the other side. Yet it is not ambiguity (indefiniteness of thought) but rather ambivalence (coexistence of thoughts). Nor does it betoken equivalence (leveling of worth), but rather respectful rank ordering (non-invidious hierarchy). That's doublethink.

Now doubletalk. Believe me when I say that *nobody* knows where our thoughts come from.† Surely mine are not of my making. No more does anyone know how that comes about which indeed does happen next: the meaning-cloud that presses to become manifest succeeds in entering that realm between subtle thought and solid thing, the realm of the word. That transmutation of thinking into talking, though a second mystery, *is*, in fact, more nearly *our* doing, one of our humanly defining efforts: concentration.

When invested with speech, dreaming gives up its aromatically intimating dreaminess to interpretable plotting. So too, when translated into language, does doublethink surrender its pensively signifying thoughtfulness. Yet there is a way of saving pre-verbal meaning, that inchoate apprehension of truths, a way of speaking that fits doublethink—doubletalk, what else? Its sentences, grammatically parsed, tend to display the "adversative" conjunction *but*, signal of a mental recoil, or the exclamatory adverb *No!*, sign of assertorial reversal. ("It's thus-and-so.—But consider also . . . or "That's how it is.—No! there's the other side."††) Its propositions, logically analyzed, tend to be paradoxes, self-contradictions, self-cancellations. Yet logic is not to be despised as a lady of easy virtue for yielding to the brute force of these facts: the world's real paradoxicality and truth's actual self-limitation. In sum: The way things are may sometimes become intelligible when logic, wisely, gives in.

Of course this double mode has given me a way of life and a mode of mind:‡‡ No fence-sitting (since double-think plants you firmly on both sides), and no prevarication (since doubletalk continually pulls you up short). But no, there's also plenty of intermediate indeterminacy and playfully lusty lying—a flanking approach toward comprehending a pervasively duplex world, a world that sometimes flashes fleeting signs of covert wholeness.

E.B.

*Although I'm no believer in the brain-mind identity theory, this metaphor from neuroscience appeals to me: synapses are non-touching junctions.

† Frost, "Directive." Frost has forgotten that in the tale of "Ali Baba and the Forty Thieves," as told in *Thousand and One Nights*, there were only thirty-seven oil jars with about-to-be-deep-fried thieves in them.

‡ Delivered by the Pythia, the high priestess of Apollo, who was then and is now known to have been sitting on her tripod over a rock fissure emitting psychoactive fumes, particularly ethylene gas (*Clinical Toxicology*, April 2002). For me, real facts are facts, but apparent implications are only apparent. Perhaps the high priestess got high to cope with the incessant mundane inquiries, but her great world-ordering replies were too worldly-wise, too shrewd, even weaselly, to have had any inspiration but sober ingenuity, perhaps her own.

§ A very early reader of this manuscript, Alexandra Wick, a recent alumna of my college and a fine participant in our fourth-year great books seminar (of which I was a co-leader), requested some more overtness. I saw her point but had misgivings, since these pointillistic thinkings seemed best served by a "the-less-said-the-better" mode. Now one way to express a reluctance to explain while explaining is to be concise. Yet the effort came to four paragraphs. Oh well, *stet*.

† Neither those in the profession of philosophy who follow neuroscience, nor those who resist it, that is, neither those persuaded that mind is identical with or emerges from a subserving brain, nor those who repudiate physical determinism, and least of all those who think the two explanations can be made perspicuously compatible.

†† An example: Freedom, it has slowly come to me, is our most humanifying mode. But No! When thought out, isn't it a condition of insubstantial vacuity, a predicate for terminal vacillation? Both at once and the more engaging for it.

‡‡ Not ever a *lifestyle* or a *mindset*. Not the former because my life is not a fashion option, not the latter because my mind is not a mold of refrigerated jelly. While I'm at it: I never *process* my experiences, since I'm not programmable. Humanly put: I strive to acquire the habit of dishabituation, in short, to preserve the spontaneity possible to souls.

1   ABROAD

The past is all Europe-tinged, Germany, Greece, England—all aroma and lost world. The present is America, the practicable now, real involvement. Where's the future? I'll find out before long.

My model: Athena, who was nice even to the Furies.*

*Aeschylus, *Eumenides*, the one Greek tragedy I think I get.

On reading the Greeks, any (classical) Greeks: They were just like us, only more so. Could it be that the more of us there are the less soul is available per person? But we populists are not supposed to go there.

Late realization: My (very non-exclusive) attachment to the Greeks was, along with plain glorying love, a declaration of independence from my "context," my determinative circumstances. In graduate school I felt my fellow German-Jewish refugees, who were, one and all, studying *Germanistik*, to be embodiments of historical determinism—though then I didn't even know the terminology. But first I fell in love.

Hymn to Hermes: "Memory, mother of the Muses"—
sounds commonplace, but bears in it a whole esthetic
theory: Memory-images are the matrix of art. The memo-
rially transformed past furnishes the matter of poetry.
It is neither a creation nor a projection, but rather it is
Muse-generated. And Muses are divinities.—Early Greek
wisdom, perennially reverberating.

There's a great scholarly kerfuffle about "barbarian"—
whether its use by the Greeks is derogatory. Well, yes, when
they hear its onomatopoeia, its barbarian babble, "bar-bar-
bar," and no, when it just means, as it clearly often does for
Herodotus, "the others." Great comeuppance: "Gringo,"
the hostile South American term for gibbering Anglos, is
derived from "Greek," as in "it's Greek to me." What goes
round, comes round.

I love those syncategorematic Greek gestures: the
men . . . de shimmy of Greek.*

* Syncategorematic: words that have meaning only together
with others; *men . . . de*: "on the one hand, on the other."

What ruined the romance of my first (and only) profession, archaeology, for me: We pieced together meticulously and laboriously what some house-slave handled as
a whole and knew as a matter of course: What broken pot
did this sherd belong to? Where did the master go to piss?
I was young and longed to learn what no one has ever
known as a matter of course.—Still do.

Ominous oracles happen when the gods find a mortal
whose nature is up to their divertissements; Oedipus was

born not only *with* but also *to* his curse. It's a case incapable of moral construal. *His* murder, *his* incest, but *not his* doing, as he realizes a decade afterwards*—guiltless guilt.

There is a late but immense compensation (the Germans say *Wiedergutmachung*, "making well again"): He goes with enormous, renewed authority, with regained and redoubled dignity not to his death—he is beyond mortality—but to his nihilation.

Where? To Athens, whence, some generations on, Orestes too will come to be relieved of *his* curse.

Congenital culpability, sanctifying annihilation, redemptive Athens—tragic perplexities, probably meant to leave thought awestruck.

* Oedipus at Colonus.

Paul, being witty. We're on the phone, somehow talking about women's physiques. I say that any quondam Greek archaeologist (myself) knows that women are built wrong: Elegance is in broad shoulders and a slim base, as any Greek amphora of a good period will testify. Women look like pears. He: Yes, they're part of a procreative pair.

The Germans, with their gnarled aptness, speak of a *Sitz-im-Leben*, "being ensconced in life," or even "sitting pretty." Sometimes, lapped in circumambient acceptance, it seems descriptive. And then, unexpectedly, it turns out we're skating on thin ice, and "landed in the drink" is more apt.

If you're a non-practicing bilinguist, the retired mother tongue tends to pop up draped in a valance of quotation marks—a sudden window on "abroad" and a catalyst of musings.

I don't really like my native tongue, klutzy and complex, boorish and prissy, violent and bureaucratic. Yet it has that *Umlaut*, the *ü*, *blüten*, *glühen*, *kühlen*, and *Glück*—and its dropping back from pursed-mouthed, poignant *ü* to way-down crooning *u*: *Über allen Wipfeln ist Ruh.** It's the linguistic analogue to "the other Germany" that home-sick emigrants used to invoke.

* Goethe's most famous lyric: "Over all the tree tops there is repose."

My folks, the Jews, do tend to be smart. But in exculpation it can be said: when they're dumb, they're doozies.

Brits too: They have the Anglo-Saxon style, but when they're vulgar—oi oi oi! Viz. Benny Hill.

I know some Brits who despise American-style civility. But an insincere inquiry into my day is way better than an intended slight to my being—such as I've heard issued in English common-rooms. (To do them justice, Americans were exempt; those transatlantic boors were known to be fragile, to boot.)

One of two functions the English have in my life: 1. as the land of that literature wherein I'm most at home. 2. as the country of customs I least go for: I'm not incommensurably un-Anglo-Saxon, but when on English ground, I'm very precisely a non-Brit. I'm for: talk first, introduction thereafter; raise serious subjects with anyone anytime; talk shop *especially* at parties; sink class differences in commonalities; regard rudeness not as witty but as socially clueless; and above all, positively, acknowledge casual American gregariousness as the proper facade for dignified reserve.

Once more, the English: the titled nobility generally isn't up to much, but when an aristocrat by patent has nobility by nature it's purely poignant.

Generally, the ancients paid the world the compliment of thinking it abysmal, and my contemporaries abrogate its depth by terming it complex. They lived with grand gravity but small mastery; we live with reduced dignity but huge potency. Would I want to be retrojected to antiquity (gender-change included, of course)? Not when I need my glasses changed—and, come to think of it, what would I be reading?

Where really do I live? Sometimes I seem to me overburdened with allegiances: Berlin and Brooklyn, Greece and Israel, above all America and the college. When the waters of imaginative memory run high, they all buoy me up together; when they subside, I'm high and dry, nowhere. So blessings on the burdens—really billows—of plenitude, and on a land that looks kindly on divided—no, on shared—loyalties. Here's how it is: Did the contingency arise, my country might ask me to surrender my life—but not my history.

2   ACTION

Most cunning is smart but not wise, but there *is* a wiliness that is wisdom's executive mode.

Coming out, taking sides, being bruised in the world's battles, is conducive to moderating our extremism and to honing our articulateness. Of the hovering ironist,* the narcissistically withdrawn "beautiful soul,"† Gottfried Keller says:

> *Wer über den Parteien sich wähnt mit stolzen Mienen,*
> *Der steht zumeist vielmehr beträchtlich unter ihnen.*

> Who vaunts himself above the parties, face afrown,
> He mostly stands considerably farther down.

* Kierkegaard's—absurd—view of Socratic irony.
† Hegel's figure for a conscience stymied in its dealing with reality by fear for its own purity.

We say: "In this life you can't achieve what you want because it's full of contingencies, emergencies, pressing duties (and we don't have servants); what's more, life is full of opportunities you don't want to miss out on (and seizing chances is our success story)." However: if you end up not having done what you meant to do, it means that you didn't mean it. Or you didn't have it in you; pick your poison. These—not really meaning to and not actually being able—are overlapping but not congruent notions.

Action, intention-guided behavior, cannot, *ipso facto*, be spontaneous. Candor, purposive speech, cannot, *ipso facto*, be guileless. Being oneself, appearing as one is, cannot, *ipso facto*, be accomplished. When young, I agonized over these impossibilities, ascribed them to inhibitions, inexpressiveness, shapelessness. It was a relief to learn that they were just the human condition, and that good intentions worked well enough in the world of fellow humans, who mostly don't even want so much expository accuracy; those who do, see past facades to something of the truth.

Two types: I. Outside—surefooted competence; inside—faltering inadequacy. II. Outside—surefooted competence; inside—sanguine assurance. Which is the better leader? It depends on the tonality of the inner state. In Type I, is it the siren of incipient failure or the ring of acknowledged human limitation? In Type II, is it the boom of empty self-boosting or the trumpet of charging self-confidence? In the right key, either type may be willingly followed, but the merged sort is best.

In public, I'm lacking, but totally, the organ for clocked competing, for the race with a nano-second finish, even for the genteel saunter of a Mayday basket competition between lugubriously drooping tulips upheld by stiff greenery and gorgeous, provocatively blooming production numbers. Yet in private, I'm capable of being competitive as hell in arcane, covert contests, in which I'm often the loser, the accepting loser—before a judge who is incorruptible precisely because she's an interested party. In sports that's called "personal best."

Life's full of incident, especially if you stay home and read and scribble.

Once more: I lack the taste for competitive sports (though I used to watch the America's Cup when it was done in boats manned by agile sailors rather than in machines worked by tech-savvy experts). My favorite old joke: Little girl at football game (another apposition of violence with complexity*—my unfavorite combination): "Daddy, why is that man running away with their ball? Can't we get him his own?"

Even Pindar's beautiful boy-boxers, celebrated in Greek too complex for my American classics education, are just nothing to me, though once, Pindar goes straight to my soul: "Ephemerals: What is anyone, what is he not? The shadow of a dream / is man. *But* when comes a god-given gleam, / a lustrous ray is upon men and a suave time."† The "but" saves life from that ephemerality, from mere dailiness; suddenly the sallow passage of our questionable being glows. But for one boy throwing another?

*Which now turns out to be brain-damaging.

† *Pythian Ode* VIII, this one for a boy wrestler, Aristomenes. I've spent quite a few hours absorbed in producing the perfect translation. No way.

Ever and always: when authorities resort to power, they've lost authority.

I was a fiercely, irritatingly "pro-active" dean in my day (having after all some tincture of the Teutonic in me). My—oh so false—hypothesis was that I could manage mess by forestalling it, not realizing until my seven years were up that that's a provocation: the more you take care of, the more solicits your care. But then the college was my baby (it had, to be sure, an extended family of care-takers),* and I joined the mothers who don't really mind changing diapers because it's a way of being close. The notion that the world can be, as the Germans say, *bewältigt* (meaning "managed, overpowered") is ludicrous. Yet an uncared-for world is unlivable,† like Socrates' famous unexamined life. So: the world must be ministered to and life must be examined. It's our charge to see to it that there's world enough and time for both.

*We eschewed the title of "administration" and lived its meaning: "ministering to."
†Nothing to do with existential *Sorge*.

WISDOM FROM THE SEVEN-YEAR'S
DORMITION OF A DEANSHIP (1990–1997)

Engage with the world and it's wall to wall emergency, meaning crisis management is the norm. People who have agreed to elevation into the active life (read: deans) and then perhaps tend a little (don't I know) to look down on those who, uncalled, just carry on—these action figures, these busy heroes, should remember: It's no use squashing emergent pests, those verminous complications (read: screwed-up kids, hepped-up bureaucrats, etc., etc.) made by essentially innocent fellow humans who crawl out of the supposedly well-caulked woodwork of the structure—unless there are also humans who just live in the house, those indispensable participants of the unemergent, even-tenored life, the ones who actually carry on wakefully (read: as fully conscious inciters, meaning as teachers, rather than as sleep-walking preventors, meaning administrators), whilst intrusions are being repelled and diversions diverted. Lesson: leave these distraction-removed, project-absorbed private citizens (read: colleagues) alone—in fact, protect them; they're living the life you're continually trying to restore. *And* do that without overriding their sense, and the substance itself, of participation in governance.

Decision-protocol, very useful when dithering: Tell a friend: "Heads up, it's go; tails, no go." Let him toss the penny: "Sorry, came up tails." Say to yourself: "I'll be damned if I'll let a penny run my life; I'm going." Bought my ticket, mind at rest.

Of commodities people tend to contribute what they have in overplus, of care often what they lack and want themselves.

Money-raisers: High thinking with head in the clouds gains a wan smile, same with feet on the ground collects a hefty check.

Seething inside is no sign of strength, and hanging on to time-expired causes is not a token of stability.

The inhibitors of action: pride plus pusillanimity—fear of being shamed and irresolution on top.

Bears saying twice to us, the people of the book: Internal seething is not a mode of action.

My political preference: reverential radicalism and incremental revolution. But sometimes everything has to happen abruptly, simply because things can't go on this way. It never works as planned but it's necessary, and that's the paradox of decisive action.

In a voting community there is usually a small faction of irreconcilables who maintain their position even after they've lost, when the decision-train is long out of the station. Why? Well, it may be because a principle was involved that shouldn't fall into abeyance, but more often it's to prepare the excuse of bragging-rights when things go wrong: "What did I tell you?" However—what went wrong was usually a factor unanticipated by the stand-outs. In low and middle level issues I'm for quick decamping to the winning side. But some things *should* be kept boiling until hell freezes over.

Decision-making:
impelled by impromptu impulse—50% disastrous;
compelled by cautious calculation—50% successful.

Whenever I hear (which is often) that "only if x is done can y occur," I expect that some of y will have occurred long before much of x is done. "Only if" is terminally annoying, because, if attended to, it brings small-scale (read: "effective") effort to a halt. But since its exemplar is "only if you bring on the millennium will kids read to grade-level," sensible folks don't mind it in any case, particularly since we've just had a millennium, and look what that's brought us.

Is it sufficient for greatness to be able to do what no one else can? Dr. Johnson—I'm citing from memory—was taken by Boswell to hear a renowned violinist: "Do you like it?" "No." "But it is very difficult." "I wish it were impossible." Difficulty, uniqueness, novelty, et cetera—these qualityless qualities are poor reasons for doing anything.

An agony to watch: an official pushed to plead exculpatory incompetence. Of course, inability is an excuse, but a ruinous one.

Predicting: never right about the *how* but generally about the *that*; good sense tells you *that* this isn't going to end well, but contingency determines *how* it'll go wrong. And contingency has more invention than you have insight.

Pseudo-conservatives: bullying obstruction and disingenuous practicality.

Our dean of old (late sixties), halting of speech: Some Black Panthers came to confront him in his office, or rather to consult him about the wrongs of the world. Wasn't the evil social injustice? No, he said and stopped. Then what? they demanded. "Original sin." They left bemused, I'm told. It's *good* conservative politics in a nutshell.

Some like luxurious vacancy, some prefer strenuous business, some get lost in canny computing.—Anyone for a spot of thought?

3   BEAUTY

Reading a Western rhapsody on Japanese rock gardens: I recalled the sight of an exquisite one in Kyoto and my abashed sense of its perfection—a sense of beauty with a penumbra of impending boredom. This knowledgeable author emphasized the esthetic aliveness of the arrangements. But to me the notion that minerals—placed stones, raked sand—are brought to life by refined human art is too alchemical: an environment interdicted to all entry that has become its own sole inhabitant, has developed an inorganic soul!

I'm generally immune to similistic extravagance, but once I saw it myself: The cedars of Jerusalem, in a suburban slum flowing down a concrete canyon: green flames. Incidentally, that's why in my mind Homer is not a "poet" (maker), but a "seer" (observer): because his similes originate not in him but in his world—neither in his craft nor in his perceiving eye, but in his inner one, which is what his legendary blindness signifies: an inner world, not made up but adventitious.

Beauty is supposed to help you through mental pain, and that's true if it's manageable pain. But if it's beyond that, beauty is an insult, added to the injury.

Why is canonical beauty so non-attractive, especially in women? Because the appeal of beauty is in its irregularities. *Nota bene*, *ir*regularities require basic symmetry, as accidents imply substances.

Average good looks (with the occasional god-bestowed high points, as when Odysseus glows) are a given blessing, and real, potent ugliness can be made into one. What is very nearly a curse is Helen-type, always striking, always arresting, beauty. And often all these Helens want is to gossip with the maids, flirt with the visiting prince, and see as little as possible of their husbands. They want to be married but not to whatever husband they've got. Thus Helen in the *Iliad*: Aphrodite tells her to go to Paris, who is waiting in their bedchamber. Her reply: "Why don't you go!"

Why is a small blemish felt to be a detriment to looks in those to whom we are indifferent, but an attractor in those we love, like that famous beauty spot? Well, first, conventionally, it is said to concentrate the gaze on an origin, as of a coordinate system, from which we depart for the surrounding flawlessness. But second, I think, it is a locus of pathos, so to speak, a small pity-inciting stain on a proud perfection.

Clear-cut, symmetric beauty can be vapid, deformity can be poignant—in humans. Not so in artifacts: In the Met, there's a small, well-proportioned, sharply articulated Chinese vase, milky green, *celadon*-colored. (I've read that "cellar-door" is the most beautiful-sounding word in English; surely that is disingenuous. Who doesn't hear *and see* it as *cella d'or*? I propose "celadon.") This little thing set me soaring, as artificial ugliness gets me down. (In a pottery outside Athens, set out for firing: a regiment of originally round-bellied, pretty *olpai*, classical little pitchers, each with a dent punched in its side—customized to contemporary taste by way of deformity.)

Beauty inundates or, better, envelops the soul as the amniotic fluid does an embryo or balmy air the body. Fluid circumambience is a figure for the unity of all beauty—it's all one nutrient medium, one vitalizing ether. Yes, but: Beauty is also inarticulably particular, each one thing of beauty is incomparably distinctive, hence soul-differentiating; the encounter with such a being turns the soul sectarian, closed to competition. The enigma: that what so invites the soul to luxuriate should also demand its exigent attention—release *and* concentration.

Beauty is achieved in accordance with terrifically strict standards that no one can articulate before the fact, but that can be clued out by the good sort of critic *ex post facto*, as in the analysis of a poem. Ugliness is either originally rule-less or parasitical on beauty, as I saw in that Attic pottery workshop: Take a row of pretty little jugs before firing and give them a good punch in their bellies—adds interest, does uglification.

What is more lovable than the physical deftness and psychic panache of some humanly privileged types? And they might even be crippled or not so bright.

Is a mutilated body lovable? Of course, but by looking *through* more than *at*. And perfect, somatic beauty can be repellent for want of mobile charm.

It seems, once again, to be a curse to be publicly, accreditedly beautiful; to be beautiful to someone, that's a blessing.

Why literati, cognoscenti, intellectuals, etc., have put a ban on beauty (now being slowly lifted): These folks are essentially critics. Critics must deprecate, while beauty demands reverence—worshipful regard. Critics must also domineer, that is, sit in judgment *over* their object, while beauty requires submission *to* it. Which doesn't mean that the "*O, que c'est beau!*" school of exegetes did better.

From the *Phaedrus*:* Beauty Itself is sheer visibility, the Form of sightliness. That means no canon, be it of harmony or symmetry, can define it. But it also means its antithesis is not ugliness but *drabness*, unsightliness; in German *Unansehnlichkeit*—the quality of rebuffing sight, inherent dullness.

There *is*—who hasn't seen it—beautiful ugliness. Is there hopeless drabness, an aspect terminally deprived of vision-inciting glow? Or is everything potentially beautiful? Consider that this conception of beauty is *not* of the "beauty is in the eye of the beholder" type, but locates it in the object, so our visual apprehension can't endow an object with beauty. But neither is beauty derived from rules of construction or a canon of criteria. So, while "beauty is visibility" does not tell how to produce beauty but only how to discern its essence, it does seem to imply that some objects and scenes are simply unbeautiful, scannable but not Visible.

What is this Visibility that differs from ordinary, ocular observability? Socrates explains that while the forms of thought-objects are dulled when embodied, Beauty alone is itself manifest; because it is Visibility Itself, it can appear among visibles as "most manifest and most lovely." Beauty then is a Form that does not lose its "looks," its "aspect," its "form" (Greek *eidos*, Latin *species*) when it enters the realm of sensed objects. It makes sense: In the world of visibles, the form of Visibility itself *appears*—not as an Instance but as Itself.

*Plato.

Once more, in brief: Socrates cuts through all the babble about beauty: It's incarnate visibility.* So beauty is not *in* but *to* the eye of the beholder. *The* maxim of sound world-dealing: *Objectum specificat affectum*,† "The *object* particularizes the feeling"—not me.

*Phaedrus.
† My adaptation of the scholastic rule: *Objectum specificat actum*.

"*De gustibus* . . ." Heavens, no! *De gustibus* super omnia *disputandum est*.

4   BOOKS

Why read fiction? Fiction extends the territory of factual life in extent *and* in depth. I mean that after each novel I've absorbed, my imaginative universe has been augmented by another world, another map has been added to the atlas of life.

But this quasi-spatial *extension* of reality can also morph into an *overlay*, into a fourth dimension for the all-too-solid real world, a "meaning" dimension, so to speak. It draws our 3D reality out into layers and layers of fictional planes, through which our dense but dimension-lacking being gains resonance and reference. Example: There's Homer's Nausicaa and her younger cousin (by three millennia), Tolstoy's Natasha. And real girls resonate to them, and their girlhood references them, and even the brats show glimmers of their deep ancestry—so to speak, of course.

People come as types and as individuals; it depends on one's viewing distance or standpoint. From far enough off, it's just one species. Great describers, mostly novelists, know how to stand at all distances at once, and their figures are at once incomparably unique and representatively universal. (I think I got that from Vico, but now it's mine.)

Real life: Homer, Bach, Jane Austen, and figuring things out.

P.S. And glory be, a contemporary: Marilynne Robinson.

Was there ever a great novel that was not, somehow, centrally engaged with theology or suffused by faith? Even the novels of Jane Austen, who seldom looks on clergymen but with a wicked glint in her authorial eye, glow with faith—even or especially they.

Dostoevsky's chapter "At Tikhon's" in *The Demons* was suppressed because it was too scandalous: It contained an account of Stavrogin's great crime that consigns him to a life rent asunder, and without which the novel is unintelligible. Nowadays nobody is scandalized, but the chapter mightn't have been written to begin with because it's too determinate. Indeterminacy is regarded as more sophisticated. A great mistake! Good and great novelists don't shrink from climactic explicitness. Evil needs explicit facts, or it becomes atmospheric titillation, a messy mystification.

There are works, mostly books, I neither love nor respect, but I do admire, in the original double sense of "wonder at" and "esteem." They are, to my mind, willfully wrong-headed, even mean-minded, but, in their brilliant novelty, they are a wondrous reflection of the plenitude of our souls' rampantly negative capacities: wonderfully cohesive misinterpretations of being by the exercise of originality, wonderfully seductive occultations of ordinary decency by the intention to gain depth, wonderfully serendipitous corruptions of language deriving from irresponsible virtuosity.—A long-winded way of saying that there is an interest of attraction and an interest of repulsion, and together they haul in the world's differentiated fullness (a.k.a. diversity).

"Confessions" are, in the beginning of the genre, autobiography dignified by reference to the confessional, then made enticing by revelatory frissons, then trumped-up seductive scandal (in order: Augustine, Rousseau, "True Confessions").

Bad endings in life and in fiction: In life, even the most apparently irreparable catastrophes are eventually encapsulated in daily living and carried off into the past; in fiction it all has to end pretty soon and quite definitively. Merely entertaining stories have to conclude in culminating catastrophes for the baddies; drifting off into the foggy future is flabby fun. Seriously appreciable fictions make such provision for the *exeunt* as the logic of the tale calls for, mostly good for the goodies, bad for the baddies. What's intolerable is the arrogation by a mediocre writer of the dignity of despair, a usurpation of pessimism, co-opted for promotion into the ranks of "serious writer."

Great books can be less than gripping. My two candidates: Calvin's *Institutes* (self-explanatory) and, believe it or not, *Don Quixote*, a scrawny old geezer with an overwrought imagination, who's the archetypal liberal (as seen by the other side)—goes around the world unnecessarily rescuing maidens while joyfully bloodying heads and breaking bones. And having carried on like this through 126 chapters, he recants! As I laid out in an unregarded little article, he's the aboriginal post-modern with an an-erotic persona, but endowed with scores of analogical applications.

Definition of post-modern literature: more fun to write than to read.

Idiot question: Are Homeric epics fact or fiction? (It drove Schliemann to tear up Hissarlik.) All great fiction was fact sometime, somewhere, somehow—all unbeknownst to the poet, who needn't have got it from life. Surely, the Trojan War happened, but why necessarily at Troy?

Poetry is radiating concision, prose braided expansion.

An author may wonderfully skewer a social sin, but not if she shares it. So in *Mrs. Dalloway*, she of the title is a terminally snobbish woman presented as she looks to another such. Hence you get a subjectively sympathetic delineation *and* an objectively repulsive depiction. So you're neither here nor there, and Woolf admirers like that.

The very being of lyric poetry is compression radiating connotations. Loquacity is the very opposite of poetry; it's gaseous speech, non-coruscating and disjoined. (In chemistry they call such gas "inert.")

Really helpful: Here's a great writer you'd like to get to the bottom of. So read three biographies: They all agree, his mother was cold and controlling. Hence, first book: He never made human connections. Well, of course. Or, second book: All his life he had one affair after another. Well, of course. Or, third book: He found a woman who was both erotic and maternal, and though he had many affairs and never made real human connections, he was, it appears, faithful to her for all his life. Well, of course, sounds like Odysseus misconstrued.

All these backward inferences yield *absolutely no explanation* of the victim's thinking. For some apples rot on the tree, some fall off all over and some ripen and are ready for picking—all from the same tree, though often we don't even know which tree that was.

Illumination during a charmingly silly lecture by an English literary light, on T.S. Eliot's *Wasteland*. (What is it with these highbred Brits with lovely heads of hair and bad teeth, that they allow their intellects to go to seed?) He said with unassailable assurance that to understand a poem you had to study its genesis, what skins it had shed. To savor a meal do you have to look through the garbage for the peelings that were tossed out? Anyhow, Ezra Pound evidently made Eliot remove an opening section on Boston's brothels, and what then became the opening was "April is the cruelest month." I didn't need to know about the Boston removal to see the point of this beginning: the revocation of Chaucer's English spring: "Whan that Aprill with its shoures soote*. . ." Suddenly the poem assumed gravity, but *not* because I knew about the suppressed brothels and speakeasies.

* Sweet showers.

Barry and Gretchen Mazur and I were driving in the vicinity of Bordeaux, when, under the impression that if it's a Great Book I'm in love with its venue, they told me, whose mind is hardly ever on Montaigne, to close my eyes. When I was bidden to look, we were turning into his place, Chateau d'Eyquem. There, in the tower to which he retreated from his family responsibilities, I saw painted high on the joists: "There is no reason which is not opposed by an equal reason." Add to this from *On Repentance*: "The world is a perennial see-saw." You'd think he would be my man.

Not so. It's mere observation, and nothing follows for further thought because nothing precedes by way of ground. He leaves it where it begs to be gone into. What I really like that's to do with him is the (now unaffordable) Chateau d'Yquem he made from the grapes of his vineyard—the only wine I've ever really tasted and can tell apart from Manischewitz. But to describe this golden wonder I haven't got the connoisseur's vocabulary. For some years it was a birthday gift from Jasha and Dodo Klein. So much for autobiographical anecdote; it's underwhelming.

Epigraph, *Middlemarch*: "'Inconsistencies' answered Imlac, 'cannot both be right, but imputed to man they may both be true.'"* I would expand: not only "imputed to man" but to everything—my new-found Heracliteanism. Long live inconsistency rightly understood!

Eliot is a wonderful citer of quotes, but if all her own observational *obiter dicta* were culled and collected, I should go out of business, all my scribblings being *de trop*.

* Johnson, *Rasselas*.

A great question in Plato's *Philebus*, which gets to me, is: *Is* there a time for pleasure, since desire not yet fulfilled is painful, and once fulfilled is gone? *Middlemarch*, that philosophy-fraught fiction, answers: There are ". . . divine moments when love is satisfied in the completeness of the beloved's object."—Of course, there *are* moments of pure contemplative satisfaction, when desire's pressure is stilled but its pleasure is not abrogated, indeed perfected, by fulfillment.

Novels, those world-extensions of the imagination, have enumerable godheads, at least in my pantheon, and masterworks in my library: Eliot's *Middlemarch* and Austen's *Persuasion*. The first is the most acutely intelligent, finely observant knower of least and largest souls and the detailedly knowledgeable mistress of her worlds. The second is, in her loving skepticism, the maker of a second paradise, a counter-world of only intentionally blemished elegance and deliciously flawed humanity. (It's my personal hypothesis that Heaven harbors similar settings and beings, a view legitimized by certain spectacular celestial events which revealed that the heavens once teemed with fascinating wickedness. Details by Milton.)

What of Tolstoy's *War and Peace* (which contains more lovably interesting people than *Anna Karenina*), with its panoramic sweeps and microscopic insights (troop movements and psychic motions)? Well, I don't know Russian, while the complex glories of English are my adopted home, so for all his detailed exposition of humanity, it's a Russian humanity and, for all my absorption while in it, a little alien.

And what of Fontane, who writes as an Austen ana-logue—the only German writer of whom I have that experience—in the elegantly skeptical dialect of my birth-place, Mark Brandenburg? But then there's the twenti-eth century between us and the use its capital, Berlin, my hometown, was put to. It's not a reservation I ap-prove of in myself—he was least of all responsible—but it's ineradicable.

And finally Mann's *Joseph* novels, whose German is a miracle of Teutonic circumstantiality combined with Nietzschean lightfootedness, which never disappoints, in-deed ever exceeds, my expectations of a denouement ex-quisitely carried off. I love the Joseph story as my own for an offbeat reason. Its meticulous antiquarianism has the magical aura of my childhood's bourgeois appointments: a bust of Nefertiti in my father's study, furniture with touches of antique elegance, Joseph himself as a look- and feel-alike of the indulged, beautiful, quick Jewish boys with whom I went to school after the ejection of Jews from the *Volksschulen*. Mine was in any case a godawful place: Fräulein Pfefferkorn, a Nazi* with her primer about how little Hans saw the *Führer*; I was slow to learn to read.

*In all fairness, the young teacher was probably clueless; this was c. 1935.

Why are novels more consistently *interesting* than life (if not as agitating)? Because in a good fiction every early incident is a foreboding, is a later event in the bud; every-thing is *folgenschwer*, "has consequential gravity," as the Germans say. In other words, the present of a fiction has a *real* future, while the present of life has an *unreal* future, a truly open future (thank God for both). And that's why a second or seventh reading of a well-loved novel is still so engrossing: you're watching—what you never get to do in life—the present in the light of the future. Example: Dodo meets Will in Rome early in *Middlemarch*. A good reader will *guess* the outcome then and there; a repeat reader will *know* of all the complexities that go into it.

Why should my heartbeat become palpable from anxious anticipation? Why worry? I've read it before and know that the scapegraces and heroes (and especially the heroines) all get their due. In any case, it's only a fiction. But that's *War and Peace*.

Reading Henry James: Reticence and discretion make for much unnecessary complexity and that in turn can make for a good novel—but a long, laborious read of which few details adhere to memory.

Again, Henry James, *The Golden Bowl*: He swathes his people in gauzy draperies of wordage. Yet the harsh truth is that at critical moments (perhaps meant to fly by), they say things of a crude bluntness such as real people rarely manage. In fact, the hard kernel of all the hinting circumlocution is usually vulgar: money used for manipulation. And the *aide-de-camp* and go-between, Mrs. Assingham, is a moralistic panderer with a noisy conscience, while the eventual heroine, Maggie, is a manipulative minx, dying to let loose what she's in decency obligated to keep within, and so to unleash a household Armageddon. Who'd want to have tea with these people? And yet—it's an absorbing tale, somehow. Moreover, it raises an entrancing mystery of fictional making: How do characters accrete such independence as to go their own way, against their maker's intention?

FIVE TESTS OF GREAT WRITING

Here's the first test of fine writing which is, *mirabile dictu*, also a mark of a writer's limitation: When characters are so alive and kicking that they play a trick on their author, cast loose, get away, circumvent their maker's apparently intended judgment. Examples: Marilynne Robinson's Reverend Boughton reveals himself as a greater egotist than Robinson means him to be; Henry James' Maggie Verver turns into a real Machiavelli behind his back; George Eliot's Dodo Casaubon is in fact of less intellectual stature than Eliot imputes to her. In fact?!! Yes.

Here's the second test, which is, on the contrary, a mark of a writer's virtuosity: When real evil is not vaguely sketched in the air but is courageously, concretely there. Examples: Dostoevsky's (censored) chapter "At Tychon's" containing Stavrogin's crime; Paul Scott's full revelation of Merrick's complex perversion.* It isn't that evil is *ipso facto* harder to delineate than good—probably just the opposite—but that most novel readers have no matching experience for the writer to appeal to.

Here's the third test: Every villain of a great book has his redeeming moment, of pathos, kindness or self-knowledge. Examples: Milton's Satan, who once "stood stupidly good"; Eliot's Rosamond Vincy, who once opens herself to Dodo. This finding of the "sweet spot" in an acrid being takes imaginative grace.

The fourth test: A real writer, like an omniscient divinity, knows what happens after the tale is told; so Jane

Austen in her letters tells that Mr. Knightley moves in with Emma to calm her father. Writers who don't know what happens the day after the novel closes don't know their story.

The fifth test: A great writer brings off culminating scenes and doesn't cut to the aftermath and funk the crux. Example: Thomas Mann's climactic recognition-and-reconciliation scene in the *Joseph* novels. Great writers have reliable virtuosity.

Raj Quartet.

Irony: Mann brings it off by his huge power of linguistic discrimination, physical description, psychic discernment. But not quite. And that's because he doesn't love his fictions as God is said to love his creatures. This all-noting, fault-including love is what irradiates the heroes of the greatest writers (Austen, Eliot, Tolstoy).

Reading *War and Peace* for the—maybe—eighth time, which is, like all the others, a first time: This time it is a meditation on history, not, however because of those infuriating history-intrusions or that story-contravening *Second Epilogue* (where a nation's fate is determined by a summing of infinitesimals, human minimals, into an integral history, a calculus countermanded by the novel, in which no human being is a mere item). Rather it's that this time fat, dissolute, sleepy Kutuzov and his wise passivity, his confident fatalism stands out. Still, I wouldn't particularly want to have dinner with the old slob. I'm for stringy Anglo-Saxons, meaning Lincoln, also a faithful fatalist, but in more shapely format. That's because I'm an American, or better, an almost-American—by choice rather than birth.—No, that's not quite right: first by fateful accident, *then* by steadily growing inclination.

Great books can bear a great deal of implicitness; a significance-laden text earns the right to leave much unsaid; aside from being in any case a necessity, it's even an enhancement. It is what we talk about when we have a book in common. But the complement is that the lesser books should be as explicit as the author's thought is capable of being made. Little writings have no right to long subtexts.

Jane Austen: Mordant love, much like what God must feel for his creatures. *Middlemarch* is still the greatest *English* novel (because of the Russians) that I know. That's because *Mansfield Park* is incomparable. I mean it, though I can't explain it. Well, yes, it has to do with the elegant simplicity of heaven versus the involved variety of earth—except that her heaven is full of essential humanity.

Since making preference lists is an indefeasible (though naughty) human propensity, here's mine: *Middlemarch* is my seventh favorite book, the first Six are all by the same author.

I wish I could tell for sure (I sometimes think I can) which writers are deep *in fact* and which are deep *by fiat*: "I must be deep, so let me add a basement."

Learned at a conference: Some authors are their characters' God and smile upon the creatures benignly, if at all possible (my paradigm: J.A.). Writers for the *New Yorker*, on the other hand, pull out before their client-characters can possibly be content with their construction; these are more like delinquent contractors. And some literary types are their fictions' employers—they put them to work parading ideological placards. Glad I went.

Why "poetry," like "originality," "creativity," "doing the right thing" is on my list of raised-eyebrow words. Here's a poetic poet: "How do I love thee? Let me count the ways"*—then comes a terminally hyperbolic list, very poetic, unsustainable as a mode of life. It's what I realized over the years about the true poets that spoke to me, the unpoetic, unoriginal, uncreative poets: They didn't "make" a thing; it *came* to them.†

For people who live by the imagination, there are, to be sure, moments when desire gets ahead of envisioning, and then a chasm opens between imagined and existent being. But at times of lusty inwardness that leap from mental to real seems to span so little, so negligible, a distance as to be a superfluous move. And yet in that "but for a little augment"‡ lies the largest miracle, the miracle of existence. Incidentally, logicians notwithstanding, to imaginers, existence *is* a predicate, a modification of being—an increase for the Here and Now, an irrelevance for the Beyond and Eternal.

* Elizabeth Barrett Browning.
† Recall: *poetes* from Gk. *poein*, "to make."
‡ Somewhere in Mann's *Buddenbrooks*.

Would you believe it? Call number for Bibles: B.S. Tin-eared system!

Why are comic writers often conservatives, viz. Aristophanes? Because they see the world as blessedly resistant to managerial reason, and individuals as intractably recalcitrant to being rectifyingly shifted out of their own type. But stubborn coincidence with one's own paradigm, indefeasible adherence to one's template, is itself funny and becomes really comic when it exactly figures the human mean. So, moreover, conservatives tend to grateful reverence for the way things are, and the human mean is the way things mostly are. And since they think that the world is not rational, they know it's sometimes tragic (tragedy being what reason can't fix), and so they like to laugh, and, if they have the genius, to make others laugh.

"Comics" are not comic, and to me, not funny, and the stand-up kind should sit down and abate their unwitty carping and mean harrying of the current quarry.

The great comedians, however, are great lovers of their land and its language: Aristophanes was a patriot and—one might almost say—*hence* a great lyric poet. Or Jane Austen—well, here's the end of her last whole novel, my favorite:* "She gloried in being a sailor's wife, but she must pay the tax of quick alarm for belonging to that profession which is, if possible, more distinguished in its domestic virtues than in national importance." Was there ever a more high-toned hilarity: "if possible," forsooth! And domestic virtue trumping national security!

* *Persuasion.*

How Thomas Mann, the most ingenious writer I've read and the most satisfaction-giving, falls short: In the record library of the sanatorium in *Magic Mountain*, presumably a compendium of Europe's music: no Bach. It's a selection that could have been made by Nietzsche: Bizet for Mediterranean sunniness and Wagner for voluptuous northern murk. I've never much liked going to the beach (sand in the sandwiches and sunburn on the nose), and I have no ear for sophisticated luxuriating (eros *in extremis** in the music and alliterative ejaculations in the libretto).

* *Tristan and Isolde.*

Hans Castorp, male hero of the *Magic Mountain*, engages in *regieren*—"governing," a form of internal world-policing. Myself, female heroine of my own unwritten life, am duty-bound to "housekeeping," a form of psychic home-making. Hans is at a disadvantage: hasn't lived long enough, read widely enough, had friends—not would-be gurus—enough. But Mann needs him, his "problem child," that way, or the seven years on/in the Magic Mountain wouldn't have eventuated. Mann himself left Davos soon enough.

Terrific book: Burgeoning imagination plus ultimate indeterminacy—*Alexandria Quartet*. Great book: Huge scope and ultimate clarity—*Raj Quartet*.

What makes the Muses withdraw, nay, abscond to Olympus? You've said it (that is, I have, really Jasha Klein* did): People being "creative."

* (1899–1978), Dean of St. John's College when I came in 1957.

In novelists and essayists social or linguistic cleverness can be an embellishment (if that's the sort of fiction or nonfiction it is); in philosophy it's a cause for suspicion—*especially* the linguistic kind.

Urban house values: "location, location, location"—but the basement has to be dry. Lyric poetry: concision, concision, concision—but the stuff has to make sense.

Iliad: gravity and grandeur—tragedy; *Odyssey*: subtlety and fantasy—comedy. Longinus* says the former belongs to Homer's maturity, the latter to his old age—a second tale-loving childhood or a later, lighter, more subtle know-how? In old age, men and women grow more alike: old Homer's *Odyssey*, more than the *Iliad*, is *my* poem, a poem for women that could have been written *by* a woman, as Samuel Butler thought.† His putative authoress is Nausicaa, a likely enough choice. This terminally charming, very clever girl falls in love with the middle-aged hero on sight. He is charmed and touched, but goes home to Penelope, also middle-aged by then—which is why I too love him.‡

* *On the Sublime*, 1st cent., C.E. (?).

† 1897, 269 pages; irrefutable proof producing no conviction whatsoever.

‡ Nietzsche, for once, gets something right in the gender realm, if only by the way: "One should depart from life as Odysseus did from Nausicaa—more with a blessing than in love" (*Beyond Good and Evil*, n. 96).

Homer's genius: the modulation of mood through metaphor.

Why do fictions have moral weight? Because they live in a fictive world in which confusion and indeterminacy are remediable conditions, and action is never a done deal but imaginatively reversible. And that encourages us to undo deeds where in fact they arose—in the imagination. Hence, reading novels is—besides much else—doing moral problem sets. Moreover, you can look up the suggested right answer in the back of the text, its conclusion. Indeed, time is so telescoped that you can learn the outcome of a decade's slow but fine grinding of the gods' mill by turning a hundred pages with one fingering clutch, and so try to forestall it.

"What would, what should *I* have done?" is the singalong descant of devoted novel-reading.

Some sessile souls study the same text all their lives—*e.g.*, Scripture, Spinoza; Kant's *Critiques* (or even just one), Wittgenstein. But they often come out with skew-whiffy notions, more off the wall than if they'd been wool-gathering (example: Dr. Fischelson in I.B. Singer's "The Spinoza of Market Street"). You have to look up, cast loose, and go on—if only to get an outside, a panoramic view of the book that's your scripture. If you don't surround it with a defining beyond, you will eventually lose sight of its sense-ensuring nucleus.

"Mystery" is a misnomer for the suspense genre borne along by the deliberate clue-strewn withholding of one resolving fact. The right way to read mysteries is to find the chapter, normally the nearly-last, that gives the solution, and be done. Whodunnit? Who cares? Why artificial suspense, when they're natural enigmas?

Is all reading in need of interpretation? Some books need no "inter" anything, they find their seat in the soul, no, its pleasure-center, directly and repose there, immediately at home. Then interpretation is a brain-wracking infelicity. Why go on when you're home free? Example? Any novel by John Buchan, especially if Greenmantle's in it. He's blissfully pre-PC, hence gift-grist for the morality mill.

Superciliousness doesn't take as much artistry as straight regard. It's no news that the sober appreciation of an orderly life is harder to carry off than its send-up.

I want my fictions to have at least as much heart as I have—more. And my heroes to have the dignity that makes their pathos heart-rending rather than pathetic. So the outside-in constructions of post-modern writing induce diagnostic interest but leave no affective residue in me.

Books prematurely "thematized" are books conclusively stultified, since the effort by which they're brought to life by the reader is that very determination of their topic (not textbooks, of course, they've got the subject encased in their title). In great books you have to work through the whole to begin to think out what it's about. Example: Tell me the theme of the *Critique of Pure Reason*, and I'll tell you how far you got in it.

What nonsense comp. lit. is: like sitting between two stools, comparing the everyway incomparable. For 1. you can't compare two items unless you're first focused on them one by one, and 2. you shouldn't just assume that works are even comparable across their own worlds, beyond "where they live." (I don't mean the real-life cultures of their authors but the imagined world they've spun.) 3. You might consider whether there "are" literatures, comparable as entities, wholes—since that's the assumption for comparing them in parts. No wonder the terms are empty: *the* hero, *the* X narrative, etc. It's even worse for lit. crit., which ended up with the books removed from it, displaced by latter-day sociology.

Once again, because it preoccupies me: *Middlemarch* is the greatest English novel I've read: psychologically hyper-acute, philosophically luminous, socially full of insight—and it meets my ultimate criterion for greatness. Its villain, in this case, the incarnation of unfathomable negation, Rosamund, has her moment—just a moment—of almost-redeeming grace: "He said yesterday that no woman existed for him besides you."

But then, in a realm beyond, there are Jane Austen's Six (particularly the last, *Persuasion*), and it's a much smaller earthly venue, a much sparer wisdom, a much greater attention to the constraints of elegance and the inhibitions of propriety. It's like earthly comprehension versus heavenly perfection, like a wise woman's exegesis of Life versus a minor angel's gossiping of life, gracefully and sedately, lovingly and impishly, in the antechambers of the Throne. Since I think—I can't know—that I belong to that minority of humans who would actually enjoy heaven, and would, like her, not be bored by the monotone of the angelic choir, I put her there, off the human hierarchy. (This isn't exactly lit. crit, I know.)

Once again: Great fictions regularly get away from their authors: Satan is grander than Milton can admit to, Dodo is more limited than Eliot means her to be, Maggie is a nastier piece than James intends—or maybe not?

Middlemarch, Chapter 74: She writes of the first worst moment, the one "that contained that concentrated experience which in great crises of creation reveals the bias of a nature, and is prophetic of the ultimate act which will end an intermediate struggle." Mostly that woman knows everything, but here I have a cavil: It's not the first but the second impulse that is indicative, when revulsion, shame, disengagement—all the attendants of deep disappointment—have rebounded to love and loyalty. The notion that crises and first responses are revealing is risky. No, the depths take time to work themselves back up after a collapse. First reactions are merely reactive, ordinarily human—that is, they revert to human nature in its physical-nature analogue mode. We are body-like beings immediately and psychic selves only on reflection.

Which is the final hermeneutic principle—deep reverence for the great ones or a sober sense of their mere mortality? Both together. *In* their company we're *of* their company.

A megaton novel is a statistical problem: what's the proportion of matter to verbiage? Is every sentence pregnantly fraught, poignantly expressed? *Middlemarch* is the gold standard.

Some writing is honest in following the vagaries and wanderings, digressions and intrusions, of the composing mentation. Here language is the agar for culturing thoughtlets and sprouting tangencies. Don't I know. What's more: you can turn the subject, the writer, into the object and then going on and on is the candor of candor, since about yourself honesty is never terminal; it has no last term.

But what I most respect is not *honesty*—candor in the subject, but *truth*—getting the object right.

The art (and miracle) of great fiction: verbal pinpointing of particularity—spare discontinuities (few words) inducing ample continua (rich pictures).

How to read different difficult texts: 1. Pester them until they open up. 2. Leave well enough alone and think along a parallel path. Both in turn.

It is a relief to those of us who have no faith in novelties how soon the "cutting edge" is just a blunt old table knife, and that the "forefront" of anything subsides into yet another link in the chain of a post-hoc foreseeable development.

Keynes: "Prediction is difficult, particularly concerning the future," implying that it's easier for the past. But not so; take the more iffy part of evolution: when you're looking at the present as an outcome, then every organism looks like a result, and every feature finds its *practical* reason; even if it's just pretty—that too will have had its survival value. Yet here's what no one can explain: Why the whole complex caboodle happened to begin with and at all, and why, at any juncture, organisms came on this solution rather than another, imaginable one.

Moreover, while for organic nature, evolution seems to be supported by hard facts and is agreeable to good sense, for the genesis of great books, those born directly of a feeling and thinking mind rather than of other books or people's opinions, it doesn't work at all. Each book is only secondarily a *link* in a continuum, a result which is a start; it is primarily a *discontinuity*, an eruption, and often maladaptive as hell. So: take each work as a world first and forget about influence and its anxieties.* For independent spirits in-*fluence* is really in-*taking*, more action than supine receptivity, and their worlds are of *their* making. Way after, if you must, shoehorn the work with belated wisdom into a story of "literature" or "philosophy."

* Bloom, *The Anxiety of Influence*.

Phases in reading philosophy: possess, second-guess, re-express. In reading fiction: visualize, empathize, memorize.

As the sandcastles we built, shovel by shovel, were washed away when we went to dinner, and the beach was just as much a beach, so the day-by-day built life seeps away in the absence of those who lived it, and the world is just as much a world. And if we were to return after decades, especially from the dead, desuetude would have dissolved its structures, and even its most devoted survivors would look on the return with deep misgivings: the need of you has been filled in.* That's what makes Penelope the mainstay of her epic: her long-breathed, assiduous loyalty, her daily resuscitation of the sense of Odysseus' imminence; she holds his place; she's his lieu-tenant.

* The theme of Hawthorne's "Wakefield."

Are great artifacts, especially those that speak or sing, sufficient stand-ins for human beings? They're certainly more reliably interesting—no, more materially interesting, interesting, that is, by reason of their matter—because of *what* they say. More than half the interest in listening to humans usually comes from *who* is speaking. This is how it is: I wouldn't want to spend less than two-thirds of my life with the most human of products, books. But that zest would fail if there weren't a world murmuring in the background, a world of living humans, there to be joined. The notion of a library that is an anechoic chamber is plain scary.

In style, must it be eccentricity versus formalism and *tertium non datur*? Of course not; there is straight speech which 1. is capable of expressing human individuality, yet 2. observes the natural conventions (not an oxymoron, since it is of the nature of speech to have conventions, primarily of vocabulary and syntax), and 3. can, above all, capture the being spoken of: distinctive, correct, adequate.

Adjectives and nouns: It's old stuff that the one betokens accident, the other essence, the modification and the being. Here's a human application: Think of crippled and cripple, Jewish and Jew, foolish and fool, lost and loser. The first is one attribute among many: in some regard handicapped, born of a Jewish mother, occasionally nit-witted, reversible by finding. The second means "nailed to the cross of suchness." So be circumspectly nominal, but, language police notwithstanding, be pungently, tell-ingly adjectival—acutely descriptive and discreetly con-clusive. If you can.

Why for the presentation of fleshly encounters master-ful intimation is so much more sensorily evocative than "exploring" description: because I resent writers' impos-ing on me their quest for words of potent impact, but more because "processing" slews of wandering words pre-vents mental images from coming into view.

An unresolved ending to a story is a cop-out unless the author has a fully imagined resolution in mind. No mat-ter how latent, that fact turns indeterminacy into denoue-ment.

Potentiation by obliteration: that's what internal par-ticularity undergoes in verbal articulation—the smooth-ing function of language: you give up singularity for intelligibility. And yet, conversely, often a notion which is no more than the unregulated effluence of my conscious-ness comes off as a novelty when cast into language.

Really revealing etymologies: *Sprache*, German for "speech," related to Latin *spargere*, "to scatter, disperse" / *Logos* from Greek *legein*, "to collect, pick up"—the duality of language as broadcasting to the world and gathering-in of the mind, as a medium for telling and as a precipitate of thinking. *Legein* is prior to *spargere*, in time and truth.

Daily exchanges are, to be sure, more casual than public speech, deliberative or ceremonial. But the most formal speech is, I imagine, that employed in unuttered self-communing, where unfiltered literacy is allowed to reign, without boundaries of time, language, or vocabulary.

"So" is the moment's universal speech-tick (as "like" was before). "So" marks an inference. People who begin every sentence with "so" are implying that anything whatever they say is a conclusion. What is it from which everything follows? A contradiction, as we learn in logic—its first sin.

Why can't people end their discourse? Because it has no middle, which must occur for an end to come about. And why didn't it have a middle? Because, *mutatis mutandis*, it had no beginning. And how didn't it have a beginning although it had a start? Because this speech act was moved not by an articulated thought but by a periodic urge to emit utterance, give vent to the building loquacity-lava.

Machiavelli's donning of a splendid gown to read the classics in privacy has a linguistic analogue: For daily business functional colloquialism, for contemplative solitary leisure, high English, sometimes even unabashedly archaic. Do most of us in fact use choicer language when talking to ourselves than we would dare use in public?

It bears saying often: The notion that language is *tout court* for public communication is plain contrary to human experience. Mostly we talk to ourselves—and that's communing, not communication—two syllables less to show the curious immediacy of myself, the articulator, telling myself, the originator: the essence and enigma of self-hood.

Listen to babies just this side of infancy, early in the morning before anyone's up and they get really hungry; they lie or stand in their cribs and utter the most beguiling, sweetly human protolanguage. Who knows what it means or intends? Whatever it is—probably a sort of self-communing—it isn't communication, but it's surely the *fons et origo* of speech.

5   BUREAUCRATS

Our students are told: Don't talk about outside sources
or personal experiences in seminar. I countermand that:
On principle, don't; in practice, do, which means: within
bounds. Good rules are particularly exception-prone:
pure principles *need* corrupt administration. Why? Not
just because "the exception *proves* the rule," that is, re-
awakens the sense that there is a rule that *should* rule,
but, more significantly, because rules that bear no bend-
ing and principles that bear no breaching are prudence-
impervious—which is to say, badly framed. Rigidity in
administration betokens a craven lack of mettle: "If I do it
for you, I have to do it for everyone" is the cover formula
for quondam people who've disappeared into their job descriptions. If you know and have confidence in your principles, in their bearing on life, you'll eschew "a foolish
consistency" in favor of judgment, officialdom in favor of
authority, and you'll know how to make deviations more
than plausible—even sensible and comforting to com-
plainers: "Why did you let him . . . while I . . . ?" "Because you are you and he is he. Or do you dispute that?"

Administrative timidity: to load onto rule-obedience
("if I do it for you, I have to . . .") the decision that is an

official's personal responsibility. Principled action (which requires not only having principles but the courage to administer them) is always exception-receptive, because 1. principles are held by *thinking people* who should not consign their judgment to them, and 2. principles are *prudential universals* and should tolerate breaching.

Stupid rules: Never flout them, but circumvent them craftily. Even people of subdued intellect (or they especially) have that intelligence known as cunning—they're *extremely* rational animals, and good at getting around the obstacles to their reasonable self-interest. The moderately bright should copy them.

Suppose I (or someone even more trustworthy than I) regulated the weather and controlled mankind. Would it then be that "All shall be well, . . . and all shall be well . . . and all manner of things shall be well?"* No, the earth would be the venue of one compacted case of bad "unintended consequences."† What is the true name of the "invisible hand" that guides people to promote a good end "that was no part of their intention?"‡ It is the flexible *cunning* of calculation, common in both senses: low and general. Next question: What puts it out of kilter? It happens when ordinary self-serving turns into extraordinary rapacity and average individuality into corporate abstraction.

* Julian of Norwich.
† Robert Merton.
‡ Adam Smith.

Some (quasi-) thoughts are so smartly stupid, you have to belong to the best and brightest to think them up. There are whole corporate campuses to breed the type. But stupid, just plain stupid, is as rare as genius.

6   CHANGE

The idiot mantra (adopted by my window on the globe, the *Economist*): "You shouldn't [surreptitious meaning: couldn't anyhow] resist change." What but change is there to resist,* especially when it's for the worse? This is the law of the flock, all trotting toward that cliff into the non-being which is someone's else's notional future.

* There not being enough *status quo* left to make its defense worth one's while, so to speak.

It seems that great, significant change is glacial, while the hectic scampering of all the instantaneous "revolutions" dies down and leaves things—discounting collateral damage—pretty much as they were. Trouble is, the delicately fine things of this world *are* the collaterals.

One day it's all over, and people's lives morph from an acutely revealing intensity to a comfortably enfolding mundanity. Is that a collapse or a culmination? Tolstoy's *First Epilogue* has the answer: twenty-four parts of national War against one part domestic Peace, but I think for him that brief conclusion is life's distilled glory.

In my active days, my ambition was maintenance, in accord with life's universal entropic trend—things tend to degrade into mush. The rage for improving innovations usually transforms fine distinctions into gross homogeneities.

Just as it's trickier to renovate than to build, so it's harder to maintain than to innovate. For keeping things going requires continual resourcefulness constrained by care for what already exists, while starting anew is, so to speak, care-less.

Humans talk, moderns communicate, devices interface—guys confront (each with its kind). Next: postmoderns interface with devices, devices communicate with post-humans, no one talks—guys do as always.

Here are two terms that got themselves connected in my mind because they are occasionally used in proximity and excite a faint frisson of being "special" (a third such word, which ought to mean the opposite of what it does: belonging to a species ought not to be so special*).

The words are "novelty" and "uniqueness." Novelties are mass-produced items with a curious essence: newness—not their particular features matter but their being curiosities that have just now come on the market. "Just-now" is *modo* in Latin, from which, in late Latin, comes *modernus* and our "modernity": "just-nowness" as a historical epoch, the world in the "invent-and-junk" mode. So novelties are little nothings emblematic of our time.

Uniqueness† is valued as an antidote. As novelties form a promiscuous class, all things newly made for the sake of newness, so a unique thing is an inherent "one-off"— a member of a class that by definition has just this one member. Its essence includes "one-and-only-ness." Thus the last remaining item of a species, such as that Mauritian dodo, is not unique, merely alone. It seems that in the world of human awareness there cannot, in principle, be a unique being, since we are not cognitively constituted to *recognize* items that do not have a species-nature or a class-categorization. On the other hand, one might argue that every individual whatsoever, natural or artificial, is unique, since no finite observation can ever penetrate to its ultimate particularity and articulate it.

So the possession of novelty is a fugitive gain and the attribute of uniqueness a dubious distinction.‡

* However, this meaning of "special" as "particular" goes back to Latin *specialis*.

† My favorite dictionary, the *Heritage*, has a longer usage entry for "unique" than for any other word I've looked up.

‡ Except under the hypothesis of faith: All of God's creatures are unique by virtue of their individual creation.

A mess-making and a meliorating maxim: 1. We must have change; let's devise a change. 2. This doesn't work: let's fix it.

It's possible that in business any change is better than none; it shakes things up. That's the economist's "creative destruction"*—future heaven paid for by present hell. It's also possible that in a school mere change is merely deleterious; actual learning needs sedate administration. So in general: a mere desire for mere change needs inhibition, a concrete design for real improvement needs implementation.

*Schumpeter: "This process . . . is the essential fact about capitalism" (1942).

Rigidity is the enemy of stability. The former is frangible, the latter flexible. Dug in: burial-ready.

7   COLLEGE

Here's the wisdom at work in my college: We presuppose that lively expressions of the intellect are all we need or should want to know of our students' personal life—because we think of thought not in its curtailed form, rationality, but in its plenitude, wisdom, in which it extends through the soul, informed by and informing all its capacities.

The Preacher preaching to the choir (me): "That which has been is now, and that which is to be hath been: and God requireth that which is past"—a capsule description of our program of study, pre-certified from on high.

College official: "Notice that I never refer to us as a Great Books school." Why would one be proud of suppressing a glorious fact: our ability to discern, willingness to acknowledge, readiness to walk with greatness—one case where submission forestalls inferiority.

A colleague of thirty years, a little displeased: "You're a mystery to me." To me too, but I'm tickled pink that he credits me with doing it on purpose.

When colleagues evince—very mutedly—a certain irritation with the big-frog-little-pond eminence I've gathered (mostly a consequence of longevity), I say to myself, dismissively, "Their problem." But it isn't; it's mine, and the self-suppression that would alleviate it just isn't in me. And so it *is* my problem. I'll live with it; piping down in a faculty meeting just isn't in me.

There are colleagues sitting around the octagonal table in the coffee shop before seminar gossiping about some fascinating people and their scandalous doings. They're talking about *Anna Karenina*—literature become life.

Preamble to an early salary report of my college: "The work of teaching is invaluable"—a word that can, in a certain mood, be heard ambiguously: "beyond valuation," "of no value." I'm still laughing at how true it turned out to be, money-wise.

Toward young colleagues: Here's what I do, now do it your way.

Perhaps my colleagues (if they attend at all) regard my occasional distancing from the founder known to have been most my intellectual progenitor (Jacob Klein) as vestiges of youthful rebellion (at eighty-seven!), or even rivalry. No such thing, truly, but rather a sense that ancestor-worship would de-flesh the rotundity (literally) of the real man.

Our college conversation banks on the ephemerality of its detail and the persistence of its drift.

8   COUNTRY

America: What's ugly—a lot of it—is convenient and what's beautiful—from sea to shining sea—is glorious.

Scratch a cowboy, find a, likely very minor, poet—whose verses are touching in their human accessibility. Scratch again, and find a brave buffoon who affects brutality and pretends to find every injury short of fatal funny. That's because running herds of *extremely* stupid animals is dangerous and make-or-break demanding: non-stop exigency. I learned this from watching my friend Randy Kirk, a Christian cowboy (now ranch manager), not very churchy (he thinks the preacher talks too much and so he drops off), but really interesting to talk with about the Bible—at 5 AM, when he brews up a jug of cowboy coffee (the spoon stands up in it) and reads and ponders his Book—and, wonder of wonders, he wants to know my thoughts; he thinks it's *my* book. So scratch a third time and find an exegete.

Deep America: impersonal friendliness, well-regulated jostling, companionable atomism—the non-rebarbative protections of privacy.

The Star-Spangled Banner (the words by an alumnus of my college) is a pretty good emblem of how I love this country: a trivial, flabby piece so unsingable that on large public occasions like baseball games the national anthem is turned over to a lady soloist, who further deforms it with self-pleasing tenutos. This neither beautiful nor soul-erecting former drinking song brings tears to the eyes—for its connotations: safety from tyranny, liveableness in daily life, opportunity there for the seizing, a sort of glorious philistinism with its fairly reliable decencies. And for the grander side of this land's lovableness there is what was once the runner-up for the national anthem, "America the Beautiful," that sings of this continent from sea to shining sea (I've crossed it thrice in my blue bug) and of its self-aware nation, at least *intending* righteousness:

> America! America!
>> God mend thine every flaw,
> Confirm thy soul in self-control,
>> Thy liberty in law!

Should I try to rise above, to excel,* my fellows or squelch my ambition? First answer: What makes you think you've got that problem? Second answer: Of course you've got it, because in America, one large Lake Wobegon, "all the children are above average." Or does that mean you don't have it? This is a smart-alecky way of dealing with an inherent agony of democratic life at all levels. For the highest, read young Lincoln's speech to the Young Men's Lyceum. It is the speech of one who "thirsts and burns for distinction" while reverencing, as a "*political religion*," the laws of liberty and equality.

*Latin *excellere*, "to be eminent" from *ex*, "out" and *celsus*, "high."

Big question, living in a democratic republic: Which preoccupation is more risible: elitism or egalitarianism, wanting there to be the elect (and oneself among them) or wanting people to be equal (at least the others amongst themselves). To be sure, life differentiates: Some *do* better than others; it doesn't mean they *are* better. To be sure, nature has made us *even* in basic respects; that doesn't mean all-round *parity*. Why indulge either in *hybris* or in *ressentiment*?

P.S.: Has anyone ever heard of a devotee of natural inequality putting himself in the lowest percentile, or of an ideologist of egalitarianism giving up a socio-economic privilege? Well, maybe this or that martyr-type.

"Matters human all-too-human": What notion of humanity does that express? Nietzsche uses the ordinary German locution *Menschliches Allzumenschliches* in a title, surely ironically; it's what his books are *not*—just commonly human. This idea of a low humanity *appears* to be formulated by Aristotle when he distinguishes tragedy from comedy: the latter imitates people "worse"—but then he adds "than those now";* thus this low humanity belongs to characters inhabiting a comedy time, not to living humans. These texts and the double meaning of "common," vulgar and universal, signals an ambivalence I imagine to be lodged in every democratic soul: Might some, perhaps many, of my fellow-Americans be naturally low, like comedy-folk? Here's my resolution: It all depends on when and where. Take an ordinary weekend and its venues of entertainment, and it doesn't look so good. Take a time of crisis and its places of public assembly—and it's sheer grandeur, citizen style.

* *Poetics.*

A difference between boor- and high- (Lincoln-type) populism: do you see your fellow-citizens as common-vulgar or as common-human, as banal or simple, as gullible or trusting? How you see them tells how *you're* made.

"All men are created equal"—yes, in the sphere of natural and legal rights. But no, human nature is not in the class of items that *can* be "equal," a calculable condition. Insofar as it is fundamentally common, it is not equal but same; insofar as it is ultimately particular it is not equal but incommensurable. And that reflection should be the source of unegalitarian *respect*: appreciation tailored to our unquantifiable humanity.

Here are three bases for egalitarianism: 1. *theological*—we are all, equally, God's creatures; that's our Declaration. And 2. *naturalistic*—I might have abilities somewhat beyond many people and knowledge tenfold theirs, but under the aspect of eternity it doesn't amount to a hill of beans; that's from reflection. And 3. *agnostic*—there's simply no knowing who'll hold up in the ultimate pinch; that's from experience.

There is—I've been its object—a rustic gracelessness, shading into cunning cloddishness, that disables one's better judgment—by appealing to one's populist inclination toward ingenuousness. Its charm depends on which end of the performance-spectrum it's on.

The art of democratic living: conviction buffered by tolerance and tolerance buttressed by conviction.

Human equality (except when qualified by "under the law") is a democratic *postulate*, *not* a provable, or even very plausible, *proposition*. And yet, not so implausible either, since we do in fact live not so much *by it* as *with it*, meaning that we don't so often invoke it as enact it. To my mind, two human truths underlie democratic equality: 1. Whatever our distinctions may be, pain hurts all equally, and 2. We never know what fellow beings ultimately have in them.

Thus the human equality postulate with its supporting truths can probably outlast the most scandalous material inequality, because we're made equal neither completely *de jure*, nor effectively *de facto*, but ultimately *de natura*— not, however, by our positive nature but by our ineradicable natural imperfections: We hurt and rightly claim parity for our pain, and we fail reliably to measure others' worth.

It's evidently possible (I offer myself as evidence) to be a populist (in respect to people) who has a liking for and faith in her fellow-citizens and at the same time—*horribile dictu*—an elitist in respect to culture; I have only the flabbiest liking for the milder phenomena of pop music like barbershop quartets and musicals, big band and swing, folk and movement music, rock and roll, and none for its latter-day harsh morphings.—Elvis is my aberration, but that's mostly because he looks like Hadrian's Antinous.* And I don't really love Whitman and I abhor football and the Marx brothers make me yawn. I'm not just occasionally brought up short by this dissonance: perhaps I'm as much European refugee as American assimilant after all. But then, it's a free country: no one's bothered but me.

*Camille Paglia's observation; he was the Roman emperor's young lover: sulky beauty, fragile viability.

Young officers, especially lieutenants, lead their platoons from up front, issuing hand-signaled orders. But people in office in democracies should often lead their people from behind, receiving mail-sent directions— "often," because they are representatives, "not always," because they are not sent to be mere mouthpieces but to act *in propria persona*, to use judgment and assert conscience on their own, though for us.

Real Americans: didactic speech, gratuitously delivered, tends to raise resistance in them, but not if they've paid a hefty admission fee for the lecture, a guarantee of expertise.

One more reason why I love America: Got into one of those hellish merry-go-round automated phone services with the MVA—no access to a human being. What did I do? I phoned the Governor's office. Within thirty seconds, I was talking to a very sympathetic MVA official: "I'll take care of you." He did. Where else in the world?

All this American basking in self-bashing accompanied by exhortations to do what the admonisher is clearly him/herself incapable of, for example "think outside the box," "be in touch with yourself," et cetera, et cetera. Yecch. Yet, how harmless compared to transatlantic hectorings!

America is everyone's diaspora and so all our ingathering.

9   DEATH

Real quandary: Why think concentratedly about ulti-
mates of the post-mortem sort? When you'll find out
soon enough? But what if the quality of afterlife is determined by ante-mortem reflection?

Imagination of what comes next: Either nothing, which
is, *ipso facto*, not so unpleasant. Or something, which has
the advantage of not being nothing and the disadvantage of coming in two possibilities: very unpleasant or
very pleasant. *Tertium non datur*, as the logicians say: a
third possibility is unimaginable, namely that the afterlife should be plain insipid. *Re* the first: a few eons in the
post-mortem penitentiary—how long a sentence could
my badness, bad enough, though moderated by a lack of
personal format and worldly opportunity, draw?—may
pass in the blink of an eye for an inmate who has studied
the temporal modes of eternity. *Re* the other possibility,
of which I have vivid and precise pre-visions: all the landscapes whose airs and atmospheres have ever wafted by
me there for me to stroll through in their archetypal actuality; the unfraught company of companionable, cour-
teous, and witty angels; the restoration of everyone I ever
loved at the peak of his or her nature and *sans* annoying

habits or fleshly flaws; conversations that are frequently conclusive yet don't end; never-flagging interest in interesting things; all the times of the past that I've read my way into, there in their flower, but with modern sanitation, insofar as it is wanted in the hereafter; the meaning of music now so particular and so elusive, then robustly bodied forth. For paradise is exquisitely phenomenal; the place of transcendently vivid Appearance. And at its center, which is everywhere, an unfailingly responsive Person, willingly moved to laughter by my—then never mis-firing—humor and communicatively ready to impart everything worth knowing, waiting to receive it back in my own but over there never idiosyncratic language; an invisible God of gods, on indulgent terms with a horde of anthropomorphic deities who haunt his Paradise as they once did Hellas and Anahuac, and one of whom (a Greek) is my special friend.

Sometimes it seems that dying off might be a very adequate solution to life's problems. Then again dealing with seems better.

"Every third thought shall be my grave," says Prospero upon retirement. Too frequent, I think. After all, there'll be grandchildren to whom to teach magic tricks; Milan isn't that far from Naples.

The *bonum* of a long life: Passing incidents, especially mishaps and embarrassments, congeal into full-blown anecdotes. Its *malum*: you forget the facts, so truth-telling isn't even an option. Or maybe that's the best bonus.

Ignorance of the time of our death was one of Prometheus's gifts to mankind. Well, yes, but nonetheless, as time advances the mathematical probability of imminent death approaches 1 = certainty. I've been reading *Being and Time*,* and no fancy levering of death into our ultimate possibility persuades me to forego that *sound trivialization* of indeterminately futural death for the resolute facing of it at every moment. In any case, the above calculation collapses the scope of existential choice—no kudos to be gotten for facing immediately impending realities.

* A book that, once again, the closer I come to catching its meaning, the less I trust its truth.

In age you lose your taste for competition. What is the joy in besting your fellows? Where excellence is measurable, go for "personal best"; if you're in charge be *primus inter pares* (or *prima*, if you must); for your very self, don't try to be best—be incomparable. But no! trying is fatal.

Old age—to be sure, a little irascible, easily annoyed. But that's a surface ruffling; within there's a peaceful pond of amused sympathy.

I'm sorry to say that my not being seduced by the divinity status that comes from long-livedness in one and the same place is not a consequence of my modesty but of its hilarity.

I'm going to die, but not right now. It seems enough. On reading the death section in *Being and Time*: I'm full of objections. Human finitude (to be sure, our principal constraint), has absolutely nothing to do with death; if we were immortal (even if it didn't turn us into struld-bruggs*) we would still be finite; the "not now" of death is not an inauthenticity of the "They," but the gift of ignorance from the gods, which we should use with gratitude; our aboriginal *Schuld* (guilt *and* debt) follows on our original sin, which is a perfectly "ontic" (ordinary) condition of never being altogether in the right. All this levering up into ontology, *pfui*.

*The aging immortals of *Gulliver's Travels*.

The generosity of old age is easily come by: the harvest's in. But you still have to actually expend it.

In youth the body often arouses the soul; in old age it's got to be the reverse.

Watch a grand dame in decline: a terrible old age, being made the most of. High drama.

The serenity of old age: Oh, really? Well, occasionally, particularly when under observation.

The garrulity of old age: time's short, so why not out with it, all of it, the hell with shame. And behold: No one notices that revelations have been made. Nothing's safer than by-the-way confidence, because on normal occasions, social inattention is a—well, actually, saving—grace.

Is the near prospect of death terrible? Not really, seeing that what was best in this life was borrowed from beyond—and if that's an illusion my mere demise will not demonstrate it.

The blessing of old age: much warmth, little heat.

The post-mortem question—What happens afterwards?—you can't answer, and if you do, you can't have let thinking take its full course. Well, yes, but isn't that what faith is, abrogated thinking? And isn't that what wisdom is, knowing when to surrender?

After-class conversation with a terminally secular (very likable) colleague—he's left teaching to become a psychological counselor, forsooth. A student had admitted to having faith. Me: "I wonder if there is a special talent for faith, a capacity, like musicality, but for hearing the Word?" Colleague: "Eva, you can't be serious!" But I was, and *he* wasn't.

The impatience of old age: "Get to it, time's short"; its patience: "Take your time; I'll sing my tacit descant."

Forgetfulness: the rejuvenator of old age.

MEDITATION ON BEING DEAD

Being dead, not *dying*. The latter is too much a matter of chance to be thinkable-about. If we're lucky, it's sudden; if we're careful, we might weasel ourselves out of the worst *then*—by means of much strenuousness *now*. If we're unlucky, it'll be bad—this dying. Well, I've paid my dues of mindfulness—now I'll let it be, all that jogging, walking, dieting.

What is more imaginable is, oddly, being dead: The heart plummets into an abyss of bereavement at watching the thingish things of the living world closing up over my bodily place, while a visible image (my portrait in Room 12) and some invisible ones (my memory in some people) take over as, what seem to me to be very inadequate, surrogates.

The venue of my life-long work is full of ghosts, ghosts of the living departed (alumni, mostly) and the dead departed (colleagues mostly). Will I myself be such a ghost, as invisible to those then in possession as they will be unknown to me? It's not a good idea to return dead to a world that's given away my place—but I've dreamed it, walking through our Great Hall, seeing but unseen, addressing but without response; yet it was a melancholy joy that it, they, were still there. This dream ghost me is truly diaphanous, a see-through body with a time-expired soul.

To look back from a future beyond my death to a past which is this present moment of my writing: a pseudo-grief brought on by an Escher thought, a faux frisson induced by a Borges conceit. Stop it! Well, soon.

I think even a very locally-attached ghost would not come back twice: longing for impossible recognition, burdened with incommunicable wisdom, being out of place as never in life—and should there be a plaque or a dedicated place, that would only document the displacement.

Our own life snaps; even a long dying is ended by a quick quietus. But the bonds of loss *within* life fray slowly—only very gradually has the pleasure of memory entirely supplanted the pain of loss. Perhaps it's the same when you're dead. Slowly you are acclimatized to the thither, now your hither home (not too hot, I hope), and slowly you're released from trans-funereal bonds. For while in this present world we have memory as the quasi-sensory surrogate for perpetuity, in the other world remembrance is expelled by eternity; it's all *now*, and nostalgia is inapplicable.

Enough. What's my warrant for these fantasies? My *bona fide* agnosticism. I *really*, *un*skeptically don't know, so anything is possible, including nothing, of course. But where the mortal mind cannot touch down on solid ground, it may disport itself in subtle vapors.

Enjoyment without that residue of avidity that infects most pleasures (the paradoxical longing that a desire be satisfied and last forever)—that's the relief side of old age. The down side is that you're exhausted a while before the pleasure is.

Socrates' central wisdom: You have to teach yourself occasionally to reach Paradise* here and now. He calls that "learning to die."† Then you've already lived your afterlife and don't need proofs of immortality—which we have no way to know of, though we may hope.

*Which the Greeks located in Hades, an underworld Heaven, with a reservation for heroes, poets, and philosophers: the Elysian Fields.
† *Phaedo.*

There are continuous and also continual people: the open-enders, incrementalists, life-squatters and also the closure-seekers, turn-on-a-dimers, life-occupants. The former are incarnations of modernity who move without finalities, stream without breaks, live wholly in life: human fluidities. The latter look for closures, hope for disrupting moments, live partly out of life (as Socrates puts it: Practice death!): not-just-now souls.* A not-so-neutral assessment.

*Modernity" is from Latin *modo*, "just now."

More and more there are the fugue states, distancings from the world, nostalgias for things present, hauntings of daily venues by the aroma of bygones: the world without me, I bereft of the world. What is needed is diversion, the diversion of world and work, just what Pascal and Heidegger, in their zealotry, want us to forego.

Dying *out*, fading away from having lived enough, seems to me eminently unremarkable, so to speak. But cutting *off* one's life, feeling so engulfed by suffering, so swamped by a sea of troubles as to take arms and by opposing, end them? Is willful not-being properly opposed to suffering? Well, yes, to being a suffering being, and these, suffering and being, end together, or so one expects. But no longer being is not the proper antithesis of no longer suffering; that would be being happy. So we of the Judeo-Christian West suffer from this asymmetry: We have a pretty sure way out of unallievable suffering but no reliable way into its real opposite, happiness. Could this be *the* attraction of the other religion of the Book—that suicide, rightly undertaken, assures bliss?

Why the old get willing respect: defanged (toothless) wisdom, that's why.

We, I at least, can live with a terminal postponement of ultimate truth—but I couldn't live in ignorance of certain available facts, say the result of a test that told if I had death growing within. It's a pervasive human propensity. (Its minimal analogue is picking at a scab: to leave it be is a greater dis-ease than the exposure of the wound.) I tolerate decadal psychic blackouts of my very being and need the light shone yesterday on what's—it can't be helped—nearest and dearest, my existence.

Life has an Ending and an End, a while of leaving and a moment of being gone—and perhaps a post-mortem, certainly a Here and possibly a There. The middle, the pivot point, Death itself, the End, is literally neither here nor there, supposedly everything and really nothing to me, a non-dimensional exit-or-entrance. The leaving, the ending can be prepared: Socrates took a bath so as to save the survivors trouble; some make a will, with the same considerate intentions not uncontaminated by the wish to work their will beyond their living presence. And then there's the other side, not the being gone Here but the having arrived There. Good sense tells you that preparation for it must be life-long; simple faith is willing to bet on a last-breath absolution. Provident citizen or faithful rogue—if there is a Next, will it have mattered? Maybe some of us for a few aeons, disinfectable immigrants being held in that post-mortem Ellis Island, Purgatory.

These lucubrations are exceedingly odd: I can't tell whether I'm deadly serious or terminally light-minded.

It's a little late to be afraid of death, now that, whenever it comes, it can't be said to be untimely.

10   DOUBLETHINK

"*Doublethink* . . . is a vast system of mental cheating,"*
from the fictional Goldstein's rawly realistic treatise. He
explains: "Even by using the word *doublethink* it is necessary to exercise *doublethink*. For by using the word one
admits that one is tampering with reality; by a fresh act of
doublethink one erases this knowledge . . ."

But *mirabile dictu*, doublethink is also at work in a system of mental fidelity, an admitted tampering with the
rules of double-valued logic in the interests of reality. It
requires, very exactly, double-thinking: not either yes or
no, but *both* yes *and* no. And a second supervening act of
the same sort eradicates the falsity of contradiction and
turns paradox into truth.

What then *is* the difference between cheating doublethink and truth-capturing paradox? One is intention:
lying self-manipulation versus candid receptivity. Lying is,
as those expert liars, Gulliver's whinnying Houyhnhnms,
know, saying "the thing which is not"—when you know
the thing that is, of course. That's the *doublethink* of the
newspeak sort; those hyper-virtuous horses would have
added a conforming province to Orwell's "Oceania."

But there *is* a double meaning to doublethink, and the second is mine: "the power of holding two contradictory beliefs simultaneously," to be sure, but *without* positively knowing "the thing that is," though with a settling conjecture concerning the thing that *is more likely*. It is the capacity to see the other side, not to glance *at* it but think *through* it. So, down with doublethink and up with *doublethink*!

*Orwell, *1984*; see the footnote to my title.

Levity : gravity :: frivolity : seriousness :: life's holidays : life's holy days.

I'm a radical moderate sitting on the fulcrum. Both extremes have truth, but one probably ought to tip the scales a smidgen: slide a little in that direction and so determine action. Explication: a root-moderate differs from a weasel-moderate (who shuffles back and forth about the pivot) in extricating moderation, temperance (a root-virtue) from inertness. *Meden agan*, as Apollo's temple said: "Nothing too much"; moderate even moderation. Get off the center to achieve effective determinacy.

Re elderly dispensers of *Lebensweisheit*, "experiential wisdom"—an annoying type whose every pronouncement has an equally true antithesis. And even if the preachment turns out to be the predominating truth, you can't hear that until the preacher is long dead. So let everyone be his own wiseacre; trust only yourself, and that very suspiciously.

Doublethink *in nuce*: Coherence is the test of truth; systems are the rack of thought. And: Contradictions are the invalidating scandals* of rationality; paradoxes are the vital principles of truth-telling (Heraclitus).

* From Greek *skandalon*, "offense," also "trap laid for an enemy."

Alternate title—of this screed and my late life: "Yes, but, . . . no, and yet." *However*, I don't feel at all waffly. For if truth wasn't calling in from somewhere beyond my ratiocinations, there'd be no reservations, no second thoughts, aroused in my recalcitrantly slow self.

"The Road Not Taken": I like the side roads, preferably dirt or best, a grassy sward—not to go off on my own, but because the paved highway, though often congested, isn't necessarily the true mainstream. Off-route is often where reality is stationed.

Depth of intellect and naiveté of heart seem to be mutually dependent soul-features. Inquiry that doesn't issue in simplicities and faith that doesn't develop complexities, subtlety that doesn't collapse into unities and innocence that doesn't long for illumination—these are dangling suspensions, not sustainable positions.

My cockroach lady: That Eleatic stranger in Plato's *Sophist* speaks of the battle between the Gods and the Giants, the dwellers among pure, transcendent Ideas and the aborigines of cloddish, sensual earth. Mostly I'm with the Gods. However, I invited this lady to lecture.

She didn't have a philosophical impulse in her head, but had enchanting stories of cockroaches and their circadian rhythms. Ditto, a professor who talked about the colony-life of slime molds—one life, many individuals. So the moldy and verminous basement of the cosmos has its illuminating attractions, and the Giants should have research grants. (Are there fellowships for transcendence?—the gods forbid.)

The right sort of fence-sitting: riding high facing both ways, Janus-like. Albeit uncomfortable, it *is* a position, not a way of waffling; it takes inner balance.

My touchstone:

> CORIN: And how like you this shepherd's life, Master Touchstone?

> TOUCHSTONE: Truly, shepherd, in respect of itself, it is a good life; but in respect that it is a shepherd's life, it is naught. In respect that it is solitary, I like it very well, but in respect that it is private, it is a very vile life. Now, in respect it is in the fields, it pleaseth me well; but in respect it is not in the court, it is tedious. As it is a spare life, look you, it fits my humour well; but as there is no more plenty in it, it goes much against my stomach. Hast any philosophy in thee, shepherd?*

This Touchstone is the master of perspectival variation, which is the opposite of vagrant relativism. Why? Because of the focal "it"—"it" is *one* life, from several points of view.

*As You Like It.

Dissoi Logoi, Double Accounts: The Heraclitean world of tensed balances, marshalled verbally:

national	global
personal	individual
simple	sophisticated
thoughtful	intellectual
pictural	digital
wise	smart
conserving	innovating

et cetera, et cetera.

Snaffle all the rubrics, catch all the dualities, to know the more precisely which side you're on and which goods you're foreswearing. Even better: Do doublethink—no, double doublethink: straddle both columns *and* lean normally a tad to the traditional left (on papyrus), which is the modern right (in politics), sometimes the other way.

The ineradicable inadequacy of my thinking comes from its being mine, its ever-recurrent doubletalk from its being of the world, its importunate hierarchies from its being mindful of a Beyond.

My Heracliteanism: it meets my inclination, the achievement of old age, for unflabby flexibility: Heraclitus raises to world-principle the twanging tension of conjoined opposites and the proportion-preserving transformations they induce. Our first philosopher!

Is there an open mind—just open? My version of openness is ambi-valence, seeing the "strength [*valentia*] of both [*ambo*]" sides: unsettled definiteness, *not* ambiguity.

The trick of life: flexibility *and* backbone, openness *and* determinacy.

Skepticism: All the why's like ducks in a row to be popped off: Why should we live in, care for, the world? (Perhaps we shouldn't.) Why take a large view? (Perhaps squinting reveals more.) Why long for acknowledgment? (Perhaps it's too much like a Chinese meal.) Why be so determined and determinate? (Perhaps we should, like physics, make a principle of "uncertainty"—though generally extracting humanistic applications from scientific principles is foregone distortion.) So now there's a lot of dead ducks. Can we dress them?

Principled compromise, the salvific counterpart to principled radicality, is, of course, a paradox, one in which those of us who elect live dogs over dead lions, rejoice— and by which even the lions, those smelly cats, in fact also survive.*

* A saying: "Better a live dog than a dead lion."

How the world has changed (not an exclamation): Pascalian diversion was sought-out distraction, ostensible amusement. Ours is life-imposed all-too-real business, complexities that entangle us. Escape attempts end in recapture and penalties of even more time served plus fines. In short, diversion is not discretionary in modern life, but just *is* living in one's time.—Pascal's diversions were self-imposed and ours are inescapable; we live in a world of exigent necessities.—Oh, really?

"Doublethink" has a double meaning: thinking on both sides, thinking twice. But no, if you do the one, you're doing the other.

Ever and again: train yourself to deep *and* uncertain conviction.

11   DREAMS

"Big" dreams, magical visions, deep conversations, all with their indefinable eventfulness: these grand occasions impend over the next day, going fugue-like in and out of short-term memory, and repeat themselves over time like spontaneous festivities of the soul, mounted according to a hidden calendar: that golden-lacquered, red-sailed junk deep in a land-locked harbor makes unscheduled oneiric return voyages every decade; that re-materialization of *the* paradox of imagination, a timeless *aboriginal* childhood *memory*—bulrushes in a little lagoon opposite a willow-framed beach where we swam and presences dwelt, childhood intimations of Pan's inaudible piping—that drifts in when least foreseen; those intimate yet grave dialogues, in which affection and insight feed on each other, and that eagerness and occasion bring about, unexpected yet ever welcome.—That the mainstays of life should be so fugitive, not in their import, but in their eventuation! And yet so persistent.

Telling a dream is like capturing image-airs and passion-aromas by surrounding them with bold black outlines: *willfully* post-positive conformations—as the lit-critters say: narratives.

How could people turn the interpretation of their dream over to another, an expert, forsooth?—when its rhetoric is uniquely private, devised for me and me alone? But to me it speaks clearly: When I wake up, I know something I didn't know or know for sure when I went to sleep. For example: Where's my heart, really?

12   FEELINGS

Unintended aversion is much harder to swallow than well-founded dislike.

Not to be wanted in particular hurts; not to be wanted on principle amuses.

That hanging, which so wonderfully concentrates the mind:* So too does a tragedy (not the staged sort) clear the mind—the mind afflicted with the overwrought complexities arising from a surfeit of well-being, in which material prosperity is slighted and psychic perturbations are magnified.

*Samuel Johnson.

Ineradicably irritating: the jabber about the Western suppression of emotion by reason—well, what the jabberers think reason is. But was there ever a real thought (thought by a real human not in the calculating-machine or information-technology mode) that wasn't paired with its proper affect?*

*That goes even for micro-thinkings, such as are expressed in conjunctions, be they connective, concessive, conditional, or contrarian: *and, though, if, but.* As ever, see William James: "We ought to say a feeling of *and*, a feeling of *if*, a feeling of *but* . . . quite as readily as we say a feeling of *blue* or a feeling of *cold*" (*Psychology,* "The Stream of Conciousness").

Kindness, a lovely experience to undergo, has this curious limitation: It can give relief, comfort, ease, but not happiness. Why not? Because it seeks our soft spot which wants a tender touch, while happiness makes straight for our energy which craves a firm encounter.

To me it's a continual wonder why professional counseling in fact often works. Students complain, in fact all the world does, of not being treated personally, that is, as friends. But of course, that's just it: what professionals have are textbook checklists and experiential patterns; they see symptoms to tick off and paradigms to match. And just therein lies the comfort and the help—more immediately than it would in affectionate sympathy. The comfort is in fitting into a tried, true and tractable class, the help is in known efficacies. In other words, troubles fit into categories and that calls for an impersonal approach. But not all troubles. Why not? Because some grief, though rooted in the simply human soul, has highly specific efflorescences—which means precisely that generic wisdom can't assuage it; it's a grief to be lived out, not a problem to be solved.

You—I—can't love people for just bearing a burden (presumably the deity can), but you have to love them for bearing it nobly. So those who could, even would, do without sympathy are the ones to get it most readily. Chalk up another one for life's unfairness, a poetry-producing feature.

I copied this out from Marianne Moore's works: "The deepest feeling always shows itself in silence." She's right, because feeling flees expression, being *essentially* inarticulable, meaning you can abstractly name it (love, reverence, etc.) and analogically describe it (deep, pure, etc.), but you can only convey a stripped-down simulacrum even to the most resonant fellow-soul.

But then she adds something I think I miscopied and now enter as my own qualification: "The deepest feeling shows itself in *restraint*, if it's to announce itself at all." Restraint keeps feeling undissipated, indeed compressed and yet not suppressed.

So why not just keep the affects you care about to yourself? Because 1. no expression means less poetry ("less" rather than "no" because *pace* the world, not all poetry is self-expression). And 2. you'd bust.

The heart may be charitable and the head understanding, but if the sensibility doesn't cooperate, kindness withers.

Why do people talk so much in defense of the gloriously inarticulate emotions against that monstrous regime of Western rationalism? They've misplaced the proper defendant.

A lovely complementarity: idle affect attracts its investing shapes and fallow delight acquires its defining target.

Epicurean wisdom: ration pleasures so as to prolong their intensity. Better: Let her rip, then take a rest (that is, go to work).

Who wouldn't rather be the object of vapid courtesy than of crocodile compassion?

Two views: 1. Prolonged longing, like all deprivation, is debilitating. 2. No, semi-starvation makes you sharp-set and long-lived. Another one of those simultaneously true antitheses, and, like Heraclitean contradiction, incomposable without making, like the contradictions asserted in apophantic (chastely declarative) speech, everything into nonsense, or, like those framed in logical terms (such as p • ~p), always false. The logic of speech is more restrictive than its wisdom. Nonetheless that wisdom depends on logic insofar as its truth comes about precisely in outrunning logic's validity.

I've reluctantly discovered a new kind of obligation: to be aggressive in kindness. Meaning that some people who recede because they feel hurt need to be pursued.

The number-line passes from negative to positive through zero. Does the affect scale do likewise? Is there a null effect between pain and pleasure? Yes, for an instant; but no, time-extended affectlessness is not a non-pathological option. The pivot time called relief is first a great pleasure and, after a while, not so much evanescence of feeling as a withdrawal of attention to one's affective state and a refocusing on good work, a regaining of engagement in which neither pain nor pleasure is any longer very prominent. But that's exactly the worthy absorption of the soul in a worthy project that Aristotle calls happiness.* I think it takes latter-day philosophers like the Epicureans and Stoics to bring forward the self-contradictory notion that there is comfort in affectlessness: *apatheia*, the feeling-free state; *ataraxia*, the upset-free state. Well, maybe for the terminally weary, like Odysseus' sailors, "There is no joy but calm."† But for the still energetic, happiness is, paradoxically, *self*-oblivion—and that's way above *non*-feeling.

* *Nicomachean Ethics.*
† Tennyson, "The Lotus Eaters."

While things are in suspension, while acceptance of our offering, plan, interpretation, is as yet undetermined, we play possum to ourselves, supine, indifferent, coolly unconcerned. And when there's an outcome, a vote, a ruling, a decision—then we learn how much it mattered.

Practice pro-panic, apotropaic* apprehension, to face the event serenely.

* Greek: literally "turn-off," prevention by magic, as by the eye-trinkets that ward off evil.

Grievanceless grief—utterly without recourse: when people hope for responsive affection and get impenetrable courtesy. It's cruelty holding itself harmless.

I'm for wide sympathies and narrow tastes—where the center is dense, the purlieus can spread.

Em-pathy, "feeling one's way within"—often illusionary. *Sym-pathy*, "feeling along with"—usually limited. I suggest *peri-pathy*, "futzing around feelingly"—mostly achievable.*

* Induced by Clifford Geertz's thoughts on anthropological understanding in *Local Knowledge*.

The body goes off on its own in attraction or revulsion. Then there's a point of decision: do I give it its head or deflect it? Do I accept its affirmation or denial, allow or forefend inclination, bear or escape distaste? Well, disinclination is our sensibility sitting in judgment—probably inexpugnable.

When you've "expressed" your feelings, you're empty, yet nothing's "there" until it's articulated. That's a dilemma of the embodied soul. (Someone might prefer "ensouled body," but then it's perception, not reflection, that's to the fore.)

A rebuff wounds my feelings? No, it's more the shame of having misgauged the occasion.

Leave it alone? Not possible, worry it out.

I drink my half-cup of French Roast (my only Francophile propensity*), and the Muses speak (to me, they don't sing, though happily to my Homer they do both, sing the *Iliad* [*aeide*], speak [*ennepe*] the *Odyssey*). Yet even the caffeine-induced high is an opening of the heavens, albeit a subrepted one. ("Subrepted" is a term Kant likes, for stolen, thus illegitimate, wisdom.) It doesn't last, and shouldn't. Stolen fire, even Prometheus's, needs to be soberly banked. Purloined highs are for starters, self-tended embers are for carrying on.

*Well, no; there's Tocqueville, who makes America lucid to me.

It all amounts to a round, ripe everything or a rivelled, raddled nothing, the rising and falling levels of our there-ness: mood as world-interpreter.

The complementarity of human relations is mostly asymmetric. One weeps, undone, the other comforts—distressed, to be sure, but also collected, gathered together in the not ungratifying effort to do this competently, to give not only fellow-feeling but also counsel and perhaps protection, and that while suppressing any hint of the inevitable—that's how we are—superiority the lucky one (for this time?) feels over the afflicted.

13   FRIENDSHIP

Make a friend of someone who's naturally reserved, a little stand-offish (not shy, which is, in adults, sheer self-indulgence) and you'll have found a soul of great natural sweetness.

The entrance into a true friendship is like passing through slow-opening, stately doors. People who think they can batter down the gates and overrun the position, will find the garrison gone.

Friendships based on things atemporal held in common are just better than those based on a common history—less stuck in past experience, more immune to the lapse of time—but the latter are better than nothing, for sure.

Hypocrisy, they say (actually, La Rochefoucauld says), is the acknowledgment of virtue by vice. So is routine civility the respect *indifference* pays to humanity—the baseline condition for community. Next step up: *interest*, then: *friendship*.

What interrupts social occasions more surely than laboring attempts to keep them going?

If we aren't in awe of another's otherness, if we don't feel our desire to penetrate as intrusive, if, in sum, we don't long to be a welcomed invader, yet marvel at not being rebuffed—then there isn't much to it; we're taking an open city.

Here's a lovely sequence: when you've learned of a friend's reliable solidity of intellect and *then* discover that he's got lots of occasional charm.

Tact in gift-offering: enough spontaneity to surprise receptive recipients, enough perceptiveness for ready retreat if it's unwelcome.

Fastidious friends will worry: "Am I imposing in so often asking for an understanding response?" Well, acquaintances can (and do) wear out their welcome, but friendship works in reverse. The more easily you can ask, the more spontaneously I can respond.

When a friend hurts you by an unexpected critique, you can 1. wilt, 2. doubt his* acuity. 2 is the better first option; it calms you for second thoughts.

*"He," by preponderance, is the right article for me to use. But it omits my oldest friend, with whom I lived out—in Brooklyn!—a chastely romantic European-style adolescence. Our friendship lasted through seven decades. I diapered her boys on weekends. Her husband, who doesn't make things up, told me that the last name he heard her say on the night of her recent death was mine.

Every friendship has its particular tension: the friendship tacitly known to be unequal in natural endowments;

the one in which one friend bears a distinguishing or burdensome mark; when one side is much richer; in which one friend is rising much the faster; when the friend is at home in one venue but out of place in another. The management of disparity is one of the arts of friendship.

There's really no temporal rule: With some friends, mutual confidence develops at a punctuated pace and persists from occasion to occasion; these are the friends for life. With others you are precipitated into confidential talk on the first day and then never again; these leave memory traces of mere potentiality. The world is alive with a reasonable amount of friends, but is blessedly haunted by many might-have-been friendships whose actualization would be just one thing too many.

In friendship, being just a little afraid of the other's judgment is the spice. Fearless friendship is insipid.

Admiration we receive as a wage earned, gratitude comes to us as a debt repaid, friendship we gather in as an effort brought off, but love is a "free gift" (in the redundant terminology of advertisements); not being good nor even being lovable can bespeak it. So, affection you can snaffle, thanks deserve, and respect secure, but love is gratuitous and life gloriously unfair: *"Wem der grosse Wurf gelungen/Eines Freundes Freund zu sein . . ."**

*Schiller, "Ode to Joy"—"Whoever has succeeded at the great throw of the dice for becoming a friend's friend . . ." He means a pretty ardent friendship. And this best-known German poem (via Beethoven's Ninth) isn't so great in the original either. As for the symphony, the choral last movement was—of course—a cult piece for me and my adolescent—very classy—gang of New York immigrant kinds. On my own, I came eventually to hear the first movement, or rather *see* it. (Like blind Homer, deaf Beethoven is eminently visualizable. Remember Disney's *Fantasia*?) In the midst of all the creation-welter and nature-chaos, twice, for a fleeting moment, Pan emerges, playing his pipes.—Complete enchantment, then and now. The children's version: *Wind in the Willows*, "Piper at the Gates of Dawn."

Human knowledge: The mutuality of friendship often begins with discovering a lovely litany of things in common. If all goes well, it passes through habituated togetherness to a sense of the unfathomable mutual mysteriousness of those we know well by choice.

Anthropology ("knowledge of humans," professionalized): The intrusive stand-offishness of the field-worker yields (defective) lists of differences within humankind. Unless the researcher gives in and goes native, it ends with the baffled theorist's default position: meticulous non-explanatory description by reason of impenetrable mutual alienation.*

*Reference: Malinowski.

How to becloud the calm skies of friendship in a trice: allow the veil over inner commentary to blow open. That running internal by-play has an odd feature: Inside it is a serene, silver-toned, descant—"That's how we are." Once out, it is a carping complaint: "That's how you [always] are." Open air tarnishes inner silver. And then, of course, sometimes it's not silver but brimstone, truth to tell.

A most horrible thought: to meet a real "second self"*—to have my sayings anticipated, my privacies penetrated, my affects duplicated, and God help me, my figure fully visible before me, front and back. Could we even devise desynchronization so as to talk *to* each other in turns? Science fiction tends not to be uncompromisingly consequential in following out the implications of a situation, but here a meticulously logical writer could produce abysmally Borgesque agonies of hopelessly, longingly attempted alterity.

*Aristotle's description of a friend: *alter ego* (*ho philos allos autos, Nicomachean Ethics* IX 4).

A wonderful asymmetry of friendship: To me, my friend seems my better, gifted where I'm mediocre, graceful where I'm traipsy. And wonder of wonders, though he's my better, I'm not the worse for it, not the lesser. Aristotle's friendship books* are among the world's marvels in insight, but he's wrong about a friend being an other *self*: The bright well-spring of friendship is delight—not self-delight (since self-satisfaction is about as far as I can go in self-regard), but other-delight, the sheer pleasure of having found access (I'm talking bureaucratese, trying not to go overboard while feeling, somehow, transported) to so fine a being.

It's a general phenomenon: the fleeting touch of worship in an appreciation of quality is exactly what confirms our self-respect. Conversely, folks without any propensity for reverence have no purchase for dignity.

*N.E. VIII–IX.

Cheerful friendliness is the outer effect of an internal loner-mode. It's easy to be expansive if you're sure of your welcome on withdrawal.

I'm permitted to think well of myself because I have the most unaffectedly high opinion of my friends.—It rubs off.

14 GOD

My access to the hidden divinity is territorial—the purlieus of its presence: Paradise. *That* I can figure: a place where routine is exhilarating, music is declarative, words capture particularities, appearances convey being, human poignancy is unfailing. Here is a theological question I've never heard broached:* might God be a realm rather than a crux?

*Obviously not, if God is a person—well, maybe by Newton, who speaks of infinite space as "God's sensorium" (*Opticks*).

Belief without levigating humor, reverence without affectionate blasphemy—they lack tensile strength.

Over and over, I can't understand why faith is thought to be so abruptly opposed to reason. What is even formal reasoning but a series of leaps across stepping stones, legitimized by our rules of inference that leave the bridged interstices opaque? And as the concluding "Q.E.D." is a matter of faith in the functionality of formalism, so the initial "In the beginning" is a matter of faith in the axioms (Greek: "worthy things") that have revealed themselves to mathematicians or the premises (Latin: "things sent before") that have been given to logicians. If these rationalities—axioms, premises, rules of reasoning, settled conclusions—appear to come out of us rather than out of Scripture, that surely can't mean that we find them altogether transparent, pervadable by reason without remainder, or even at all. That mysterious residue—why should we think it was not revealed to us from *beyond* by a sort of internal scripture?

A consequent surmise, very tentative: We are all, the great included, "just ordinary human beings" in a non-derogatory sense. But some have been chosen, assigned an extraordinary possession; that's a literal understanding of the notion of giftedness. It's not a distinction without a difference, because it invokes two notions for reflection: 1. There is a true Human Commonality, our ordinariness. 2. There is a Bestowing Choice at work, superimposing occasional extraordinariness, for example, of reason.

And if rump-rationality is a faith-project, the more so is plenary musing, those sessions of sweet silent thought.

Re God: If he *is*, might he not be as pleased with us for being *concerned with* him as for *believing in* him?

If God did speak to us as to Job, be it in a roar out of a whirlwind or in a whisper from within a zephyr, no matter what the message, everything would be new.

There seem to be two routes to faith: 1. believe in God and *trust* in the gratuitous help. 2. confess the need and *hope* for the entitling belief. It would have to be a very kind deity that would value them equally, but *in extremis* we count on it.

Atheism—a curious notion that requires its believer first to figure a god (*theos*) and then to deprive him of existence (*a*: alpha-privative)!

On self-inspection, I turn out to have an insouciantly choosy relation to that latter-day development of Judaism, Christianity ("latter day" to me, even though my Scofield Authorized Version expends itself in marginalia noting Christian allusions built into the Jewish part). I could see myself a Catholic for Anselm's captivating sophism or Thomas's huge intellect or Ockham's radical factuality—even a Protestant for Bach's divinity-dedicated glories, (though not a Lutheran, since their founder, for all his boorish beauty, is unforgivable). What I can't, finally, swallow is the notion of individual incarnation in general and the choice of a boy-rabbi in particular.* The former idea culminated in sponsoring that human creator and master of the human universe, *modern man*, the latter contrived to put his own people in the role of *god-killers*. And yet I can't bring myself to wish that the whole story had never happened—except for its twentieth-century denouement. And it *could* never have happened, namely if those foolish Pharisees had just *tolerated Jesus into oblivion*.

* In a reading group at the college on Marilynne Robinson's Gilead novels, I asked why, in her books, so ardently concerned with Christian faith, Jesus figured so scantily. And then this slipped out: "It's anyhow absurd to worship a young rabbi as God." It took one second for me to feel ashamed and another

to dissolve into internal laughter: "*Credo quia absurdum*," says the Church Father Tertullian: "I believe [just] because it's *absurd*." I was bringing unintended Jewish grist to the Christian theological mill. No one noticed, but then, no one had felt offended—and it was not from light-mindedness either.

When a friend who has faith seeks our sympathy, do we envy God, the greater comforter, as a rival? No, because it is a great compliment, an elevation of sorts, to be bidden to be a comforter by a believer, a kind of colleague to divinity.

A reverend skeptic, to whom doubt-raising is a curlicued delight, will, I imagine, receive smiling audience before the Throne.

A sober, true, ultimate agnosticism: What I don't know I *really* don't know, having made *bona fide* stabs at knowing: God and Paradise. Most agnostics just don't want to be bothered. You're supposed to be bothered.

Reverence is the decent agnostic's placeholder for faith, the brinksmanship of belief, one might say—"Lord, I believe; help thou mine unbelief."*

* *Mark.*

Bad-faith agnosticism: "leave it alone"; genuine unknowing: "leave an opening."

Besides the sustainable wonder induced by life's great enigmas, there are the small, sudden shifts of soul, the hairline cracks in the self, when a tiny alienation with huge implications appears: Who in the world (for once not a mere phrase) am I? Is it a mini-mood or a major insight? Probably the latter, but the live innards of the experience slip away and its husk is exhausted existentialism.

I was about to say something dismissive of the frothily ebullient notion* that you could *exist* (be a *this*, here and now) without first *being* (being a *what*, ever and always). But then I recalled: There *is* created existence out of sheer divine, terminally contingent, inventive Authorial power. Or rather there is the thought of it, gravely worshipful (though to me not quite credible). Reverend Ames's is ". . . full of admiration for existence"; to him ". . . existence is a delight . . ."†

* Though existentialists actually tend to be discomfited types.
† Marilynne Robinson, *Gilead*.

*Credo quia absurdum** doesn't do it for me. I won't believe what is totally beyond me, and, *a fortiori*, what presents itself as unbelievable. But I will let it preoccupy me 1. as having captivated a fellow-human and 2. as possibly revealing truth to someone having a capability I lack. It would not be that famous Keatsian *Negative Capability*: "when man is capable of being in uncertainties,"† a mode very close to the unresolved ironic hovering of Romanticism. It would be precisely its opposite, the ability to leap over uncertainties to faith.

* Tertullian.
† *Letters*.

If it seems as if I knew my Bible, I don't. I find the grandeurs of my own testament off-putting and the insistencies of the other one irritating, and would much rather read a long novel (Mann's *Joseph and His Brothers*, for example) than the brief text itself. But snippets stick, and my Scofield Bible Concordance finds me the source. To be sure, Ecclesiastes is, unpreacherlike, hilarious in places, so he's my favorite:

> . . . the keepers of the house shall tremble . . . and the grinders cease because they are few, and those that look out of the windows be darkened,
>
> And the doors shall be shut in the streets, when the sound of the grinding is low, and he shall rise up at the voice of the bird, and all the daughters of musick shall be brought low; . . . and desire shall fail.

Well, maybe not the last, but that about shakiness, tooth abrasion, eye-sight deterioration, pre-dawn insomnia brought on by those damned starlings, and hearing loss—right on, and expressed with a slyly grand figurativeness: redeeming self-ridicule, really.

When you accept the possibility that heaven, with its ever-one-note psaltering angels, might be even more blissfully interesting than hell, with its various figures of pathos discoursing on philosophy and pursuing the arts, liberal and fine (it's Milton's venue I'm envisioning), then you'll concede that *Pride and Prejudice* and the other five are incomparable, off the mundane scale that is surely topped by *Middlemarch*, the greatest of English novels— at least up to the middle of the last century; then there's the *Raj Quartet*. My repetitions simply register what's on my mind—an explanation, not an excuse.

Two limit-options: a somewhat fantastic faith in transcendent being burdened by ontological dis-ease or a lugubrious skepticism levigated by metaphysical light-headedness. A sober question: Is it all mere temperament, finally? No, no, no; it's the whole soul's judgment call: go with the first.

Bliss wears thin—on earth. Why? Because we're not just non-angels; we're fallen human beings, consigned to sweaty effort and by now addicted to it. (*Genesis* tells me that I, in particular, in a not unrecognizable first incarnation, was culpable.*) And then a lucky thing happened. Was it intended? Besides brow-dripping *labor* ("in the sweat of thy brow") there came to pass head-engaging *work*, and now it's more reliably fulfilling than ecstasy.

* It was, however, a *felix culpa*, a "happy fault," since it got us out of an evidently somewhat boring terrestrial Paradise into the larger world and thence made us candidates for admission to Heaven, an even greater venue. (I found, among my parents' papers, a book of names for babies; a number were marked but Eva won out, the first in the family.)

15   HAPPINESS

This is what it is to be felicitously constituted: If you like a thing once, you'll like it twice, thrice . . . If you love it now, you'll love it for good (with re-creational intermissions).

Happiness as a *condition*, that of being in possession of possessions (husband, children, house-and-garden, job) can be conceived as a dead end, a *cul-de-sac* for restless souls. Contemporary writers glory in painting it as a form of despair, especially for well-off women.* I think more robust souls might find it quite livable. Then there is happiness as an *activity*, a superlatively lively, vibrant stasis, a fulfillment of the soul in keeping with what is best in us: absorbed in good work.† To me it's Aristotle's best truth and absolutely obsolescence-proof.

*Example: Doris Lessing.
† *Nicomachean Ethics*.

To be happy when there's cause, if it's not a virtue, is at least a grace, like evincing a glow of grateful pleasure for an unexpected gift.

Luck—an embarrassing helper, invoked especially when it's needed to bring you back to the baseline and credited when you were expecting the worst and by none of your doing and for no good reason it didn't happen. Yesterday it was bottomless relief, today it's a mere rectification of a misapprehension—and adjuvant luck is sent packing: "What's luck have to do with it? I lived right." Ha!

Relief is an exhaustible happiness. At the moment of things coming right it's a very swoon of felicity, but it doesn't take long and the thought prevails: So now we're back to the ordinary, meaning to the default level. And a danger averted or a grief assuaged is thus just a forgettable disruption in a life whose main question now returns: Is "ordinary" all that great?

I seemed to me quite sufficiently content. So why am I suddenly so happy because someone said a certain thing to me? It proves that even a fairly undisruptedly satisfactory life has, *ipso facto*, a damper on it; daily, diachronic existence is indeed afflicted—perhaps even sustained—by ordinariness. We aren't made for uninterrupted, even extended joy. Aristotle thinks it's the *matter* in us that wears out; his *nous* never does—but mine?

Once more, relief from a great anxiety: No sooner has the null state of normalcy been reestablished than the bliss of unburdening is troubled by a first intimation. Now all the troubles of ordinary life, terminally irresoluble because perpetually replaced, come creeping back. I read a story somewhere, perhaps in Martin Buber's Jewish tales, of a rebbe in a shtetl to whom came a man complaining of the intolerable crowding in his hovel. Take your cow inside, advised the rabbi. Soon he was back. You can imagine the rest and the relief. *But* it's illusory relief; it doesn't last. You can't magick sweet comfort from dour misery.

Fiction amends reality: Human beings are ultimately inaccessible; well-wrought characters are patent into their recesses. The given world is finally past comprehension; well-wrought stories have illuminating finality. Life keeps streaming off; novels stay put for reliving. However, when things do work out—friends come clear, the world makes sense, life is renascent: "There's glory for you," in Humpty Dumpty's immortal words.*

* *Through the Looking Glass.*

Rule to make the world a little more felicitous: Speeches should be very brief, books as long as necessary. The reason is obvious: You can shut a book more easily than you can shut up a speaker.

When I was young, I wanted to have read everything, *nota bene*: "have read," not "read." (One cold winter, doing research in the excavation house in Corinth, I did in fact start in on—and completed—reading all those olive-green Greek-English volumes labeled Plato.*) In middle age it came to my notice that the more books I read the more were published—hopeless catch-up. Now I've given up the category of "want to have read," and read only what I "want to read"—except for papers and books sent to me by friends and alumni, which mix the categories.

* Loeb Library.

Is felicity, like Hamlet's revelry, more poignant in its breakdown than as a habit, "more honor'd in the breach than the observance?" Does misfortune cast suspicion on a happy life as a passing illusion, or confirm it as a realizable possibility? Is lost happiness worse or better than none? A no-brainer, really. Though there *are* those undauntable souls to whom every misery is a "learning experience," grist to the satisfaction mill.

Pindar again, and another try at a rendition. Recall that usually half is quoted: "Ephemerals: What is anyone, what is is he not? Dream of a shadow—man." But they omit the "but," the saving grace: "*But* when a god-given gleam comes, a radiant splendor and a honey-sweet aeon is over man." Ephemeral, unfixed, shadowy to the second degree ("dream of a shadow")—but caught in the headlight of sudden splendor, we are transfixed and dulcetly eternal. I know what he means, but I just can't say it as he does.

Why do we concentratedly worry a pimple, scab, broken fingernail? It came to me while reading of real harm: These small, obsessive self-lacerations are "apotropaic"— "turn-offs," conjuring avertings, of real excrescences, wounds, tearings—a preventative fixation on minor imperfections to assure global well-being.

Part of a happy childhood: that brown-eyed nanny who was our daily companion and, by putting our parents at a distance, made them entirely desirable beings, beyond surfeit and irritation. She had a German face, of the high-browed, squarish, brown-haired, solid, kind and candid type. She was forced to leave our Jewish household by the Nuremberg laws, but, at some risk to herself, came to see us and to read to us; I used to write in the place where she left off what she said each time as she closed the book: "*Kinder, ich muss gehen.*" After the war I tried to find her, the only German I cared about. She had died in an air raid, one of those that had sent us to our potato cellar, Jews not being permitted in the public shelters.

If you've had a happy childhood, you're always the underdog in the who-knows-life hierarchy. People, I then mutter, should fear the backlash of other people ever expected to indulge them because of their—mostly bygone—suffering. But no, my about-to-be explosions always fizzle in view of the brute fact that I really have nothing to complain about—anyhow nothing extraordinary. It's just an uncircumventable disability in the victim-of-tragedy competition.

The mark of a life in which all (well, much) is well: when you wake into a day that's a relief from your dream—and the dream was about small things looming large. I kept dreaming about my ceiling being water-blistered until it *was*: no more ceiling-dreams; mundane fact purges imagined fears. There are those who are able to sleep in heaven but must wake into hell. (It's called wish-fulfillment in the crude lingo of dream interpreters.) And those—I can hardly imagine it—who go from the night's nightmare to the day's nightmare.

It would be, might yet be, a personal catastrophe if I came to distrust the refilling of the well of affect, the renewal of feeling effected by a night's sleep or a day's work. That, from all I've seen and, in part, experienced, is the dark night of the soul: a loss of trust in the sturdiness of our passion and the reliability of our love. Trust, anxious upfront and at bottom serene, trust in my given nature or in its giver—who knows; it's the non-doctrinal, wordless prayer of the hopeful agnostic.

Paradise: the place where particularity ceases to particularize (exclude) so that, love still being highly individual (singular), we may yet love *many* beings with all our hearts.

The Ancient Mariner effect: bad luck hangs like an albatross around someone's neck and he stoppeth not one in three but two in three or even three in three and embarrasses everyone. Is this unfair? Well, was it bad luck or bad management, *exempli gratia*, shooting albatrosses? No, that's wrong; once the bird is hanging around his neck, guilt questions become moot. In his progress the old sailor is turning the pendant into a stigmatic morality medal.

Don't we know, at the bottom of our hearts, that a happy life is ninety-seven percent luck? Catapulted by catastrophe to absorbent America rather than dead in hostile Poland, or hopelessly, longingly, alien in snooty England; exchanging clunky German for supple English; casting loose from an all-too-welcome scholarly tether to be received into a gloriously amateurish college made for me; just the right age to escape mandatory retirement; just healthy enough to escape superannuated, youth-choking struldbruggism, et cetera, et cetera. So why do the three percent of good choices loom so large in my self-esteem? Ridiculous.

Passions get ahead of thought, as we all know, but feeling falls behind: Elizabeth "rather *knew* that she was happy, then *felt* herself to be so."* *My* experience, better said.

* Jane Austen, *Pride and Prejudice.*

"Famous" and "infamous" seem to be about equally insalubrious. Congenital obscurity is—if it's the kind you're born, not subjected, to—the likeliest state for sustainable happiness.

"Working a problem" and having it respond: major happiness. Yet why do I nervously, antsily try to be done? It's the fear of being taken off the job *in medias res.*

Evanescent discontinuities: glorious culminations, honeymoons of the union of thought and feeling, happiness indistinguishable from pleasure. Yet it would be a sorry folly to abrogate the sober inebriation of immersion in continuous work even for such natural highs—and for artificial ones, sheer idiocy.

In a moment of overflow I made a list of events that make life worth living and then, with a pang of fear, an apotropaic list of their implosion. Here's a short version, purged of intimacies. It's a list of supererogatory blessings, not basic goods such as: never going hungry, except (not often) by choice; having a home, and what's more, one fixed up just as I like; having safe work and enough money for all sorts of things, which moreover I don't even want; and above all, living in a good, I think the best, country.

Blessings:
Work of daily interest, interspersed with moments of grandeur.
Chance meetings, developing unexpected charm.
A burst of song from next door, descants to deep talk.
Respect gladly given and gratefully received.
Waking up to a waiting work from dreams not better than life.
Dailiness receptive to prodigies.
Physical adequacy—just.
Implosions:
Moody unease, diffuse wrongness, terminal iffiness.—

But are the last-mentioned negative subjectivities not better than real trouble? Of course.

One half of a good life: health, work, community; the other half: not to live there altogether.

Paradise: where head, heart and nether region, where admiration, love, and lust, where thought, feeling, and excitement lie down together: monkey, lamb, tiger—and where human fellowship, singular love and fiery affection meld into one.

16   HOME

Vagaries of attention: Almost four and a half decades, (15,425 pencil-calculated days, less traveling absences) have I spent in this room, my study. There are my nested Platonic solids, made of slim, painted balsa spars, and oscillating in the fan's draft. I made them nearly six decades ago: they're indestructible by reason of fragility, and invisible—until this astonished moment—by reason of belonging here. Here's an odd fact: If they disappeared I'd know right away. The whole room, and life as well, consists of unseen thereness and blatant goneness. Except for my ever-handy, fallen-apart *Thesaurus* (a gift from my oldest friend, seventy years ago) that's ever-present—it even comes on trips, for while meanings come galore, vocabulary goes missing.

The enigma of return—the house's soul has shut down and cast my things into *limbo*, the companions of my imagination have fled and *nostalgia*, "return-ache," has turned into the bereavement of really being there. An *existential* mood? No, an ordinary *existentiell**, dissipated by a night in my bed and phone calls to and from reality. But yes as well: moods do intimate ultimacies.

* Heideggerianism: "existential" pertains to what *it means for us to be*; "existentiell" pertains to features of our *concretely lived life*.

Homecoming happens the day after return, when the companions of the imagination re-enter and the ghosts of previous presences re-connect. A house left to its own devices goes off on its own and requires enticing into hominess. How often will I say this? Not as often as I've felt it.

Hominess: My house has far more hand-made gifts than store-bought ornaments. Not all the gifts are very ornamental, but they're feeling-fraught. For domesticity, sentiment trumps beauty.

There are fourteen stairs in my house; the slower I get going up, the more they get counted out as a Shakespearean sonnet (4/4/4/2); thus I arrive at my study from my sweet-gobbling break as the couplet announces its conclusion:

> So I return rebuked to my content,
> And gain by ills thrice more than I have spent.*

Some days it's Petrarchan (8/6)—less of an arrival. Can you go up or anywhere on free verse?

*Sonnet 190.

Language for being at home: "*by* myself": my own *by*-stander; "solitary": only, one-ly—perforce peerless; "alone": all-one, just one—and enough, opposite of lonely. *Sola* is the fulfilled state: Partridge,* ever suggestive (if unreliable), has Latin *solus* kin to Greek *holos*, "whole." *Can* we be together with others by going inside? Yes, if we go within to issue forth. As de-souled bodies we will crumble into dust, as disembodied souls we will communicate directly, but as we are, we shuttle into and out of ourselves, to be with-out and to be with-in, to be with others and then to be home again.

* *Origins*, an etymological dictionary.

The body is the soul's check valve; it releases built up psychic pressure by means of ex-pression, and it closes off inflowing repercussions by physical buffering. And then there's the magical moment when our defensive bodily construction goes into reverse: now all intake valve—willing receptivity.

My backyard, the Navy Yard—companionable nitwits and comradely wits:

1. Woman: "Out for a walk, getting your exercise?"—I lack deniability.
2. Muscular male running by after a day of rain and overcast: "What's that yellow spot up there?" "The sun, maybe?"
3. Black woman asking time: "Have to hurry up and get to church"—there speaks the need of the spirit.
4. On a bleak morning, the day after Obama's reelection, woman rolls down car window: "Isn't it a beautiful day!" We smile.
5. Very erect officer in mufti, out of the side of his mouth striding by me jogging: "Don't exceed the speed limit." "I'll slow down for you."

Annapolis, downtown tourists: Tourism is mobile alienation, sightless seeing. They sit with melancholy, inward-turned looks, licking putrid-colored ice-cream cones, lightened of purse and heavy of heart. As they say where I come from, "They should've stood home." (But then my taxes would shoot up.) In youth some of my most forlorn days were touring, looking at the outside of places I should have been on the inside of. Well, wasn't that a *seisachtheia* (wise Solon's institution, the "shaking off" of burdens), when I realized I didn't have to cruise the world looking at it through a viewfinder but could stay home and go only where I had work to do and so came as a temporary insider.

Two human types: It's better to come home to anybody than to nobody. / It's better to come home to no one than to the wrong one.

The life of lifeless beings: Inanimate gear, lacking (to speak with Aristotle) a principle of motion, of maturing or declining within, would, one might think, stay pristinely immobile, unlike organic beings, which flourish until they wither. Not so; once made and left to their own devices, it's all downhill for artifacts, entropically. Leave your house, and fans freeze, doors learn to creak, dust settles and water seeps, while insect carcasses make a potter's field of my home.

Parents "bring up" children, and once up they prosper for a long time on their own. But artifacts go into a repair-soliciting reverse from the moment they're made and ever after. (Animal ethologists speak of the "care-soliciting" aspect of the young, lost in maturity.) And *that* is, I think, why we become affectively involved with things; they're care-absorbers with a refurbishable mortality. Well, that's part of it; I own myriads of artifacts that contain (books) or emit (CDs) much of the companionable wisdom and beauty of the human world; they're soul-surrogates.

A friend remarked: "You live the most stripped-down life of anyone I know." He means no e-mail and such. But there's my house—utensils, clothes, mementos, pictures, papers, records, CDs, and (how many?, perhaps six thousand) books—I wouldn't call that spare living. No one has friends to spare and pen pals to do without and alumni enough to lose track of, not to speak of the dead who might be grateful for remembrance. And what of the scores of scores of life's events?—classes, memorials, celebrations, daily business, travels? Curated accumulation—*that's* my life, not so stripped down. But, to be sure, sparse in technological distraction-facilitators.

Once again, Home. My house rejects me. The nerve! It's let in ghosts, dregs of departed days. This house "that is no more a house" must undergo a ghost-cleaning, an exorcism (or I must: nostalgia for a fled life). Nearly half a century, and I don't know how things work (that's the least of it), or why I think I live here. Yet, should it go up in fire, drown in a flood (unlikely, the Navy Yard lies below), blow away in a storm, I'd be nowhere, not just without my roof over my head but without the depository of my life. Could happen.

17 HONOR

Unconscious loftiness—poignantly lovable, especially in the young.

Cultivated naturalness is to me the only imaginable appearance of human nobility, as a way of life. (Notice, emphatically *not* "life-style," with its demeaning sub-text: Our life is a fashion show.)

Does "pride goeth before the fall" mean "when the nose is stuck up, the toes tend to trip," that is, pride makes you *overlook* pitfalls, or does it mean "hubris incites the vengeance of the gods," that is, pride *asks* for it? Whether it's your own insouciance or your calling-out of the powers that be, this vice is nothing to fool with—it can break bones. But, then, there's the other pride, honor-pride, without which you're boneless, spineless to begin with.

Offense-taking is really absurd. Either the offender is a jerk and so his intentions are big nothings, or his endowments do entitle him to be taken seriously, in which case you shouldn't give him the satisfaction.

Sidney Poitier, playing a prison psychiatrist in a pre-integration movie: Visitor expresses surprise at a Negro in that position, then catches himself. "No offense meant." Poitier: "No offense taken." It stuck with me because offense-taking, mistakenly thought to express self-esteem, is actually a sign of lacking the dignity that would reflect the offense serenely back on the offender.

Highmindedness, certainly. But what about the in-eradicably childish, petulant, ignoble self? Here's a way out: To be human is to contain both ends of the moral spectrum. So feel smallness and enact largeness. I'm always first to myself, but what I love is a close enough second to make unselfishness no pretense, and what I wish to be is vividly enough present to make disinterest no sham.

To be sure, these transactions have a lot of iffiness about them because of that lurking self. But then, do I really admire self-lessness? It's a little boobyish.

Offense-taking is ignoble; be above it. *But* offense-absorbing has to have a limit. Determine when to get angry. How's it done? Discretionary temper is a concomitant of self-control. Since, like compressed gas, suppressed temper gets hotter, let it up and out deliberately and you'll get a scary effect: cool temper.

Warrior souls, albeit in civvies: who show their wounds only long after the battle is done, if at all.

Is it noble or ignoble to forgive real wrongs? There is a delicately brittle pride that cannot forget and a weaselingly elastic viability that wants it over with. In general, is the make-or-break loftiness (as of the people who walk out on a great love) or the put-up-with-it abasement (as of the better-a-live-dog-than-a-dead-lion people) more ultimately vital? Well, the non-compromisers are often counting, in the recesses of their mind, on recalcitrance being the winning strategy, and the compromisers actually have a good deal of condescension in their yielding. Probably the latter for me. The proud tend to be, after all, a little obtuse, which diminishes true dignity.

Ever and always: Hierarchy is the principle of a livable life; it makes many-directed engagement possible, for it accords each element its moment of respect without confusion about the rank-order.

Give me a middle-class kid, even a street lout, over the academic elite for glimmers of great-souledness.

Captain Dan of the Caledonian Canal barge "Scottish Highlander," to requests: "I think it is achievable"— a locution fraught with dignified prudence; I'll borrow it.

Talk of honor: Would anybody with a lively sense of shame make honor a talking point? Honor comes into play when you're in the moral narrows—not a moment one wants to be known by. Pride is even less speakable— a bottomless sense of personal worth, not something to announce to your world. In our time, to be loquacious about honor is to declare oneself a laborious simulacrum of a man of honor. Well, happily, women are anyhow exempt.

Noble—a worshipful word favored by some of my very middle-class colleagues (*Nota bene*: I think the middle class is the central class, but not the locus of nobility— well, perhaps Jefferson's "natural nobility"). What, then, is noble? (Nietzsche asks in *Beyond Good and Evil* but hasn't, to my mind, got a clue.) Was Socrates noble, was Moses? Bach? Lincoln?—or Homer who made nobility immortal? They were *way beyond*. Sometimes, by a miracle, there are real live aristocrats who are actually noble; we don't hear that much.

Nobility isn't among the traditional virtues. It has its absurdities, such as Aristotle's great-souled man who walks slowly, sedately, and has a deep voice* (Lincoln's was squeaky). It's probably an occasional characteristic—comes and goes with circumstance—as when Shakespeare's Antony sends his abandoned treasure chest after Enobarbus, who has scuttled from the sinking ship. So there's disdain in it, often. And it's sometimes deliberately tacit, as in disdaining to defend yourself or to call in a favor.

Nobility takes badly to being theorized; it becomes ludicrous as a scholarly subject. Yet, when it suddenly radiates, it's adorable (in the non-cute meaning) and invites emulation. This much is clear: It's the most individualizing of impulses and without necessary relation to a particular regime (*pace* Montesquieu†), class or political circumstance. Some young have it by nature, but in maturity, when nature has been curried by reflection, it doesn't lie quite so well, except in the inconspicuous mode.

* *Nicomachean Ethics.*

† *Spirit of the Laws.* He assigns honor, which he does not rank as a virtue, to monarchy and its nobility.

More on honor as a repellent subject of talk. As I said, it's not a virtue like justice, since behaving honorably is supererogatory. It's not "what *one* should or should not do" but "what *I* wouldn't do," not because it isn't done, but because *I* wouldn't do it—*you* might, and I'd think nothing of it. It's the inner music I move to. It's neither quite articulable *salve dignitate*, nor just "subjective"—because it follows models, live, dead, or ideal.

Being honored: the more you're a toothless tiger, the more people thank you, evidently for *having been* formidable: I want to slide under the table with late-blooming bashfulness and rear up in righteous vexation at all the misapprehension—too intent on behaving well, too befuddled at others' view of me, too startled at the chasm between being and being seen. Where is verity—in the invisible or in the manifest? Surely behind the scenes, behind that façade called a face which tells truth neither when contingently reacting nor when controlledly "presenting" (as the animal ethologists say). Yet—it's absurd—I do think *others'* looks speak to *me*.

Dignity shows itself not so much in articulateness (least of all in word torrents) as in expressiveness of bearing, gesture, face—subtle, reticent, shapely letting-on. Vulgarity is expansive because it's platitudinous (there are trite gestures), and showy because it's coarse (there is noisy gesticulation). Here's a standard example of gestural vulgarity: Woman makes an accusatory complaint and follows up with a series of offended, support-demanding eyeings of the surrounding air, nose up, chin out. Men, being debarred from the hyper-vulgarity of faux refinement, have grosser ways.

P.S. What takes more acute perception, accurate visualization, and linguistic resource than the descriptive capture of human expressiveness? There's a master of this art, to me unrivalled: Thomas Mann, from *Buddenbrooks*, his first novel, on.

Is there natural degree, *gentilesse*, nobility of being, brought out in breeding? Or is every soul originally and finally the equal of every other? Of course, the latter, of course the former, both at once. How? That's perspectival. If the angle of observation is obtuse, close up and personal (Hegel's valet's point of view, who sees his master as an ordinary man), it's the latter, but under a more acute angle, the former.

Written a while ago: "Honor is everything to the genuinely young but only a faint incentive to the old." What nonsense: from babyhood to senescence, it's pride all the way down and close to the surface. But perhaps in later life honor is coveted in the mode recommended for self-interest: "properly understood."*

* By Tocqueville, again.

The case of unreciprocated fidelity, of unilateral fealty: Do we owe it to our integrity to stay loyal or to our honor to break away? Does the final abrogation of loyalty stem from a mean desire to survive, to have the last word, or from an assertion of self-respect? Is it: "Better a live dog than a dead lion"? Or: "Better a broken heart than a cowed spirit"? I'm for survival.

The pretty intelligent person's standing is, I think, thus quantifiable:

Above the average (add all scores, divide by number tested) but below the median (add highest and lowest, divide by two). It's a way of saying: The really great are spectacularly beyond the pretty good, but the very least are well within the latters' scope, who, though above average, have much farther to look up than to look down. (But let all such quantification of human beings mostly alone; it's a conceit in both senses. Go with the Lake Wobegon principle: All the children, at least, are above average.*)

*Garrison Keillor.

There may well be an inexorable rank order of human beings in physical and psychic endowments—I wouldn't like the assignment of making it up because of the *virtus abscondita*, the "hidden excellence," as I think of it—a fineness that even the possessor doesn't clearly know of and that emerges when called up by some contingency. Then the most recessive, insipid, even slightly worthless person never looks the same again. Actually that poses a problem in daily life: this excellence of the moment tends to recede, and it's hard to remember that it once reared up.

The austere sweetness of inner dignity: natural nobility—most poignant in the young.

18   IDENTITY

Is there, when you think it out, self-love? Not if we insist on our *identity*. If we're "self-same," then the condition of love, the distance that is the requirement of attraction, has collapsed. If we have an identity, there can be self-involvement and self-aggrandizement, self-ishness, and even self-delectation, such as a worm might enjoy.* But not the self-love that Aristotle says is the condition of friendship—the self-separation, the sane schizophrenia, that gives meaning to self-respect and, on occasion, to self-indictment. Or, for that matter, to internal conversation.

* *Wollust ward dem Wurm gegeben*, "voluptuousness was bestowed on the worm," says Schiller in that "Ode to Joy"—but perhaps he's no authority on the passion-capacities of invertebrates.

Identity! Ha! I cringe at Teutonic germanicity, really— yet I'm somehow, by upbringing, German and by sensibility, deeply perhaps most deeply, attached to Bach, a Protestant theologian—when I'm also repelled by these Lutheran protesters of faith and tolerators of evil. Yet far more than German by birth, I'm Greek by choice, a pagan, captivated by visible gods and engaged by onto-logical ascents. But then again, in fate and by family, I'm a Jew, and apt always to feel for Israel, whose aggressions are driven by a "Never again," and where my prolific family lives—whom, however, I don't need to see all that often.

Again, my all-encompassing, most thoroughly lived loyalty is for America, Lincoln's America, where consanguinity—"blood of the blood"—is through the Declaration,* which I believe in ardently as delineating the best way for a political community—although its facile Jeffersonian axioms seem to me only qualifiedly true. Finally there's that minuscule institution which my old colleague's long defunct father referred to as "that chicken-shit college in a one-horse burg." (Annapolis is now totally car-congested on a weekend.) And that's where I've lived and thrived.

Am I torn apart by this welter of allegiances, is my identity a problem to me? Not a bit of it—I revel in all this personal multiplicity, and carry on without feeling at all dispersed or distracted Pascalian-wise.† Why? Because I've made out for myself, more as a working faith than as a thought-out finality, that all things good and lovable have the same ground, not on earth but beyond.

P.S. So do I have or need an identity? I'm tempted to say that Nature solved that problem by giving this multiplex soul one body by which to be "subserved" (in neuro-speak), and that's what appears on the "identification" that I in fact have. But people who "have" an identity send me thinking: If it's "self-sameness" (*idem-titas*, "same-ness") then it's not what you *have* but *are*. If it's "identification-with" ("making [yourself] the same as"), then it's not what you have or are but what you do. So give up these fancy self-fixings, go with what you love, and let that make you what you are—when you're not looking.

* Lincoln's reply to Douglas, 1858.

† Doesn't quite work. Pascal's *divertissement* had more to do with expending ourselves in amusements than in allegiances (*Pensées*, "Man's Misery").

To me (it's always "to me"—these are opinions) the way to stay ahead of the complex bottomlessness of postmodernity and the human ravages of cyberspace is to lag—presciently if I can—behind. In fact, it's a maxim: To end up essentially out front, stay selectively behind.

There used to be the boob know-nothings and the fey recluses, the willful ignoramuses and the proud taint-avoiders (Hegel's "beautiful souls"). Prediction for internet-users, a new world-mode: on-demand information consumers who butt shamelessly in and out, at their attenuated attention span's behest.

Here's a continual puzzle: Is our character *expressed* in our opinions and their consequences, or is the sum of thoughts and deeds just what our character *is*; are we a hidden substrate with discernible properties or a largely overt concatenation of features—or even just a mere collection? The latter, the Humean-Wittgensteinian bottomlessness, seems like a conclusion of logico-philosophical analysis, rather than a teaching of experience. First be, then think; first think, then speak, for God's sake!

For self-respect: be loyal to your youth, don't disown what made you who you are. Those re-makings, turnings, deliberate discontinuities, that some people indulge in—don't they devalue the preceding phases, disrupt our *bios*, our life-coherence? Sound change will save its antecedents, rash repudiation trashes them.

Can we preserve the sense of human commonality in the niche world that's coming—on the hypothesis that cyber-beings won't fulfill us and virtual connectivity won't hold us together, and that humanity will flee to small segmented realities? Yes, probably, since antique car aficionados have just this in common with hot-air balloners, pressed glass collectors with cyclists—and all knowledgeable lovers with each other: real objects and actual people, veritable "thises," *ousíai*, "substances," as the philosophers of the Tradition say: ensouled matter and embodied souls, our Things and our Selves, moving through Nature's places.

Polar people: needy and domineering, sentimental and cold, insecure and assertive, thin-skinned and graceless. Why can't they collapse their propensities and just be middlingly nice?

They say: Fixed opinions prevent an open mind. False: It's indeterminacy that obstructs receptivity—for then all distinct figures diffuse and vanish into a fog.

It's a current mantra that meaning derives from context. You can overdo that: Take the setting for the thing, the circumstances for the event, the necessary for the sufficient.* It muddies determinations not to focus on the foci but on the periphery.

* Said of conditions: *necessary*—without which the thing (or event) is impossible; *sufficient*—enough for it to be actual.

These unlimited, indeterminate post-modern personalities: it's surely a willful self-definition that allows them to go about intentionally unraveled. Isn't it a blessing to have a somewhat determinate nature and to settle into a fixed shape—whence to open up to the world?

A century of anti-rationalistic ranting in favor of sensuous spontaneity, and what do we get? Virtuality, unreal sensuality backed by ultra-rational technology.

To me, the most deleterious aspect of the conversion of knowledge into information is the abrading of the qualia, the spiky "what" of people's own thinking, into quanta, into smooth impersonal "how many," to concoct statistical super-data: true of everyone and of no one.

Our scary polarities: globe-spanning activity / screen-glued passivity; world-wide connectivity / cyber-space isolation; unforeseeable violence / office-bound number crunching.

"*Inform*" used to be the whole of what you did *for* yourself—shape your soul. Now it's what bits of crunchy mind-stuff does *to* you—determine your decisions.

Our, really, everyone's, preoccupation is (or ought to be): connectivity, instantaneity, virtuality, optionality, post-privacy, manipulability—our post-modern modes. The culpably sanguine notion is that they will bend human nature, make it accommodate them, change human being. The likelihood seems to me to be that human nature *is not* pliable but *is* degradable: our adaptations don't evolve a new species, happy in a new way, but develop masks for the old species, now sick with a new pathology.—But here I've forgotten myself: Don't I think poorly of worriers about the future of the human race?* Because they, literally, overlook people.

* Grandest example: Nietzsche.

"Information" again: that which (in the tradition) gives our thinking form or that which (in the information age) intervenes between mind and thinking—good word gone bad.

19   IMAGINATION

Here's an enigma: how does the first sight of a place that *will* be remembered come to be *already* imagination-invested?

Unimaginative writers may say that there's nothing in the imagination that was not first in the senses.* It has a smidgen of truth: Whatever we imagine we have *somehow* seen or heard. Yet, except for the "photographic memory," which is to remembrance as a documentary file (of facts) is to a manuscript folder (of fiction), nothing in the imagination is as it was first in the senses and, moreover, not everything in it was first sensorily perceived. What's the difference? Not, as those insipid boors above think, that new sensibilities are derived by blending and new compositions are gotten by rearrangement—that's just the imagination having chemical reactions.† But the imagination isn't a chemist's laboratory; it's an alchemist's cabinet where are worked transmutations by which a perceptual image "doth suffer a sea-change / Into something rich and strange."‡

What exactly is this magic? Well, what externally makes separable the figure from its affect, the scene from its atmosphere, is internally fused: The image as a representation and an affect are simply one. That's just a first apprehension in these arcane pursuits.

* Apologies to the Philosopher.
† Such as Hume details in "Of the Passions."
‡ *Tempest.*

Two resources needful to living well: Imagination enough for a refuge from mundanity in its dreary phase and words enough to give structure to affect, make memoranda of moments of delight, and formulate, seal, and deposit *ad acta* deeds best put to rest.

Is it a comforting or a melancholy thought that no person now living is the equal of the companions of the imagination? And wouldn't just a moment's restoration of their real originals obliterate all those carefully cultivated inner figures? Yet, there'd be a melancholy as of a betrayal in that, for all the joy.

An innocuous-seeming question of great consequence: Aristotle says: first image, then desire.* Aristophanes claims: first need, then the fulfilling companion.† If the latter, we're basically affective beings; if the former, aesthetic ones.

Might there be two types?

* *On the Soul.*
† In Plato, *Symposium.*

Real beings have the advantage of existence, imaginary beings of inexistence. The latter never present themselves in the mood of blah, and so they never come up stale. When they fail to meet expectations, they're renovated. When they become obtrusive, they're sent into exile. When they've exhausted their charm, they're put to sleep. The sole advantage (to me, that is) of real existences is that I'm relieved of conjuring up their so-being,* their existential rotundity. Reality self-presents.

* *Sosein*, Meinong.

How to live safely in the imagination: Proscribe all fantasy and imagine so concretely that, but for the tiny lack of a little touch of existence, the figures would pass into reality, there to meet me unembarrassed by their own impossibility.

How everlastingly strange it is that this ordinary, unscented present will be wreathed in aromatic airs by merely being bygone! And yet, what's odd about it? "Here and now" is temporally banal; "there and then" is temporally miraculous. For it's *practically inaccessible*: It is "a town that is no more a town" and requires us to "back out of all this now,"* this crowded now, which is all the time there *is* for us. "There and then" is only *imaginatively accessible*, so why wouldn't it be redolent with pastness?

* Frost, "Directive."

The unimagined life is not lived: Socrates extended.*

* *Apology*: "The unexamined life is not a livable life (*ou biotos*)."

They say the imagination is a locus of possibilities. But no, it's not a space for brainy playing with options, but rather for watching the self-presentation of actualizations, so taut as to be strumming with affect, and so precise as to be vibrating with quiddity—*the* feeling of *that* vision and no other: the involved miracle of feeling-fraught images of image-engendered affect.

Meditations on the Coalescence of Perception and Imagination: Here's a long-term preoccupation: Where's true life—in reality, imagination, thought, among bodies, images, ideas? Leave aside the last, as rarely reached. Then what's left is factual existence and feeling-fraught imagery. The first is self-presented, self-moving, hard-edged, detail-stuffed, the second summons-requiring, gauzily impressionistic, dissipation-prone. Where, then, is our true existence? Well, of course, the two realms together, in their superimposition. But they're not often congruent. And *that's* where life acquires a task and existence a direction: the greatest possible assimilation of World and Soul, by reform without and revision within—in tandem, slowly, mutually.

For me: not magical realism with its extravagances but imaginative realism, which doesn't explode daily life but extends it continuously into its contiguous realms.

Existence matters most when the waters of fantasy are low. When the imagination is in full spate, fact is mere circumstance. Is it G.E. Moore who asks: Who would not rather have the merest existent over the fullest imagined good? Most of us would—until we've actually had it.

It makes sense to attribute to fictions, which "are" in the realm of nonexistence, an especially poignant essence, that comes out the more, the less existence—here-andnowness—they have. It's a power of the imagination: to suppress existence so as to vivify essence. That's why a collapse of the imagination—often in tandem with erotic energy—induces nostalgia—that "ache for return" to one's real home, the realm of imaginative essences: "imaginative universals" (as Vico calls them), or sensory ideas, or unique exemplars. Wonderfully, this nostalgia evinces itself most vividly on return to one's—why "one's"?—to *my* actual house, that modest little weather-tiled harbor of refuge and, on rare occasion, funk hole. I unlock the door. Imagination has imploded, the life cocoon has broken, the venues to work are closed off: I am self-remote, flashes of longing beckon from the further side of a time chasm (it's the heart-sickness of a soul in limbo), until a night or two has passed, and the nothingness is nullified, the unraveled skeins of life reknitted, the threads to the past respun. And what was a double loss—the imaginative life that invests the house was never real, and now its cherished irreality is lost as well—with slow suddenness creepingly springs back. Presto: I'm home again. Conclusion: We travel (in body or mind) to experience the loyalty of our home life. And soon, the larger cocoon of duties, routines, colleagues, friends is respun.

A totally secular imagination, denying itself a transcendent source, is willy-nilly autocratic (which the Germans, my linguistic begetters, translate as: *selbstherrlich*, "oneself-the-lord"), that is, conceited, concoctive, clever, a hot-house for forcing idealets (a necessary neologism).

Imaginative writing imposes a double task: You have to find the object and devise its telling. Meditative writing is simpler. The thing is there; you tell it as it is. The compensation in fiction is that *you*, the writer, are the arbiter of what and how; in reflection *it*, the object, rules.

But no! Great imaginative writing is equally object-devoted, only its figures come forth when they will,* while thoughts invite your coming after them; it's called "inquiry."

* Examples:

1. Once more you are approaching, weaving apparitions,
   That once displayed yourself to cloudy sight.
   Goethe, *Faust*, "Dedication."

2. I thank everybody in this book for coming.
   —A.W., author and medium
   Alice Walker, *The Color Purple*, "Postscript."

Extracting the universal from the particular: thinking. Condensing the universal into a particular: imagining.

Current commentators are much taken up with the editing memory undergoes. But can't editing sharpen meaning? Especially if the editor is the imagination?

Life's a coherent tissue of rent loyalties—how's it viable? Is the condition of possibility a reliable digestive system or a sustaining faith? Whence in particular comes the steadying conviction that all the regions of the imagination, all its diverse climes and discrete landscapes, are one country? It is barely credible that I might be, as Kant claims, by my "unity of apperception," responsible for the law-governed coherence of nature, but what in me could possibly have enough unificatory awareness to make one realm of the many world-extensions and counter-worlds that coexist under the exigent spontaneity of what the Greeks called our *phantasia*,* our "venue of manifestation"?

* From *phainein*, "to bring to light, make to appear."

Ineffectual proneness, lying supine in bed but sleepless, makes us vulnerable to those betwixt-and-between states that the erect posture rebuts: fugue-states, visitations by unrealized bygones; melancholy, the intimations of the imagination's blatant non-being; nostalgia, the lost sweetness of what never was to begin with.

"You can't lose what you've never had." Tell me another: The saddest forgoings are of un-had goods—because in imagination you *have* had them—sort of.

Livable maxims: 1. Function, but withdraw as often as you're welcome to the realm of imagination, and enter, when it—very sporadically—lets you, into the region of transcendence. 2. As for real life, indenture yourself to a real program of study embodied in a real community of learning, located in a real place, and so serve, not humanity, an unlovable abstraction, but real human beings. But why "serve," when it's self-fulfillment?

20   INTELLECTUALS

Those people who proclaim that each of us (presumably including me) must be and do just as she likes, when she is and does just that, they don't like it all. It's never exactly what *they* had in mind.

What intellectuals call irony is mostly depraved indifference.

The sure way to occasion a thought-detour: Pose a question about what something is, then expend yourself in peripheral researches: How they regard it in Bangladesh, what Google coughed up for the key word, what the high school teacher said or the footnote referred to—anything to divert the inquiry which seeks the thing's ontology. Students do it as naturally as they brush away a mosquito; we all do it, actually. This needs avoidance therapy: focus on *what*, not on when, where, how. Fight the flight into circumstantiality!

Scholar's delight: expansively rectifying errors nobody's perpetrated. I have a private catalogue. Also: overtly declaring shock and covertly harboring relish at having identified a hitherto unregarded point. What kind of point? Euclid's kind: a point that has no parts.

Academics write of undertaking and—forsooth—completing a philosophical investigation. I'm for futzing around, and closing in on some thing, and watching it fall apart, and re-fortifying a position only to find the very notion of a "position" ludicrous. But from repeated waffling and settling, conjecturing and concluding, a scheme of life and a philosophical faith emerges—having, of course, in the German locution, "always already" (*immer schon*) underlain it.

To my mind a theorist who can't fix a running toilet or a sticky door is intellectually suspect because 1. some mental connections have mechanical analogues, and 2. he can't be very circumspect, look about him and make out what's up, so what's he going to be a theorist *of*? But then, an ever-so-effective practitioner of life who has no transcendental intimations is positively melancholy-making. Happily, the plumbers and roofers of this land tend to live with some faith and by some ideas, in my experience.

Why I like politicians better than intellectuals (by and large). The latter say "We [usually: Americans] are violent and greedy; we . . . etc., etc." The former say: "You [usually: the other party] are power-hungry and wasteful; you . . . etc., etc." The intellectuals are mock-inclusive; they don't mean "we" but all you yokels out there. The politicians mean exactly what they say; not necessarily that the other side is indisputably evil, but that it's them and not themselves they want to be bad-mouthing.

"Thinking outside the box," the mantra of the creativity folk, doesn't work: As soon as thought leaps out, the box expands, and they're as inside as ever. It's the same with the latest revolution, and *mirabile dictu*, with philosophy: Think what no one's thought before, and in less than a generation, it's one of the string of pearls previously strung up.

Thoughtless folk, as driven by random impulse, are pretty unreliable, but as bound by received opinion, pretty predictable. Intellectual gentry, as attached to processes of rationality, are pretty predictable, but as given over to shifting novelties pretty unaccountable. So the probability of making sense of either type is about .5.

Searching for nuggets of illumination in the outpourings of scholarship is like panning for gold in a rushing Alaska river, a chilly diversion from going direct to the motherlode: the Text Itself.

One thought: Traditional logic is to symbolic logic as steak is to jerky.

Another: The meretricious Principle of Premature Precision—practiced by academics trained in logicism. Begin with a brief and easy positing of maxims narrowly tailored to symbolic expression. Then couch propositions in semi-symbolic speech. Presto, something precise follows, which, however, when turned back into natural language, is either irritatingly obvious to good sense or off-puttingly inadequate to real life.

What a melancholy midden of forgettable intellectual labor, all our articles! Or does every effort leave its trace? Funny—I have one type of hope for most of mine, and another for much of the others'! Seriously—all this bubbling medium-weight stuff is the oil in which something deep might someday be fried up.

Influence: when an intellectually piddling notion—as it seems to me—becomes the watchword of the day and a mental mediocrity gains influence, it will be said that these were the very ideas that were "waiting in the wings," or "whose time had come." That's pure *ex post facto* reasoning. Their time did in fact come—and from that we know it had to? If we knew all the opportunistic manipulations behind these epiphanies we might think "There are a lot of impresarios involved in those stage appearances of the *Zeitgeist*." But soon it's curtains for these appearances, and the critics conduct a post-mortem. Next act onstage!

Isn't all book-learning, as the appropriation of alien thought, somehow plagiarism, and shouldn't an author rejoice in it? Aren't those intellectual goods that are principally liable to being purloined usually idea-packets or factoids hardly worth the protection?* Of course, you can't just copy things out, but nowadays that's more risky in any case. Not a rousing topic.

* Excepting results of research, that is, culled data originally arranged.

NYT Book Review: "Thanks to the dated nature of his work . . ." You're the one that's dated, with-it reviewer!

People who run themselves aground in the swatchways of life's complexities should put out their anchor, kedge off and sail on (as my skipper used to do when we ran aground on one of those uncharted shoals of that Delawarean River of Flies, the Cohansey). To get stuck in contemporary shallows and confusions, having stopped the effort to find depths and clear water too soon, wins you kudos for a post-modern sensibility, but not a joyful existence.

University press ms. evaluation: "This manuscript could have done with authorial cutting. But why did the writer not consider x [reviewer's doctoral dissertation]?"

The false presumptions of the boor-scientist: "We're way ahead, Aristotle was wrong, Newton superseded," et cetera, et cetera. The wise modesty of the true scientist: Every serious insight preserves its place, for good—as an answer to questions not asked by my profession, or as a limit case to a subsequent generalization, or as an uncircumventable indeterminacy, or as an outstripping of intuition by formalization or the converse. To the best of the tribe, the nous-scientist,* everything is questionable and hardly anything despised.

Did you ever try to get a true believer in evolution to tell you what its terms mean? Thoughtful evolutionists can contain in their mind both the fact of evolution and the opacity of its foundations.

* An English loan word from Greek *nous*, "intellect," rhymes with "mouse."

Sophisticated mandarins: *etepetete*, as my mother used to say with pursed lips ("finicky," says the German dictionary), but given to bouts of scandalizing ordinariness—not even lusty vulgarity or down-home earthiness but crude snobbery.*

*E.g., Virginia Woolf, *Mrs. Dalloway*.

I think of myself as one whose attention is easy to capture; then why does academic (professional) philosophy* put me to sleep? Because it's a self-nullifying contradiction in terms—institutionalized love of wisdom, protocol-ridden search for truth. And so its formatted humming is *ipso facto* dormitive.

*I subvert here a passing strange fact: Philosophy became a profession in Plato's eponymous Academy.

Don't use concepts to leverage your standing. The intention always shows. It's a style of young academics on the make and old ones on the defensive: didactic professionalism undercut by embarrassed overreach, derivative concepts appropriated by attribution ("as Professor X has shown us"), porridge-thinking spiced up with philo-babble.

Mark of the intellectual: lip-smacking outrage (at humans-being-human). Of the scholar: I haven't got much to add (that was twenty minutes ago). Of a social scientist: latest studies show (the opposite of the last which showed the opposite . . .).

Is nescience better than learnedness? Yes, mainstream scholarship is trained devotion to diversion. No, keep it

ancillary and knowledge is just better than ignorance.—
That's what's called being conflicted.

An old Russian friend used to say, whenever someone
announced unmissable truths as lately-born discoveries:
"Discovers America," two words that should puncture the
pompous claims for the wonders which "the latest studies
show." But then, isn't it the perpetual rediscovery of that
America, everyone's Newfoundland* and emblem of our
aboriginal ignorance, that allows us sometimes to claim a
smidgen of originality? Why deny innocent satisfactions?

* Donne: "O my America! my new-found-land" (*Elegy* XIX).
He is, however, speaking of a different lay of the land. Well,
out with it: his bed-fellow's body.

How irritating is portentous talk of Woman, her needs,
ills, wrongs! But un-ideological inquiries into the nature
of what Aristotle calls the "essential accident" of gender
are endlessly interesting. Are we less aggressive? "Hell
hath no fury . . ."! More wily? Well, Machiavelli was no
woman. More motherly? Some fathers make lovely mothers. More receptive? Some women are coolly repellent.
And if it isn't gender-universal but just on the average,
it's probably subject to change over time. I have a strong
sense that there *is* a fairly general distinction based on
our less protuberantly erectile body—maybe just a kind
of all-overishness?

Curious, editor-required, transgendering: male author
who writes "she" in places he must mean himself. To right
this discriminatory privileging, all women should con-

tinue with "he." Language-rectification impositions are demeaning to everyone, self-righteous rectifier and put-upon rectifiee.

Question put to select people of reputation by an international magazine: "What's it all mean?" All? Mean? Well, I'll try, though I'm not a member of your target group: "*All* means your oyster-world, with its entities, events, expressions. *Meaning* emerges when you scan their surfaces for significances, delve into their depths for essences, and penetrate beyond them to a ground. Shall we inquire whether our world really has outsides, insides, and yonders?"

"But," now you'll say, "that's way more than what my question really asked for." To be sure. But it had an undertone, which I'll now bring up: "What's it to me?" An answer (one not, in fact, given by the people of reputation) might be: "It's everything to and for you. For if the world is not reducible to mere noise and empty anger—not "sound and fury signifying nothing"—then there's your opening: Engage with it, launch into it, wherever it looks inviting, and it will before long—that's the reliable miracle—solicit your interest, care and love. And if you're at all responsive, you'll have your answer—though by then you won't be asking *that* question. Oh, I forgot, you weren't *asking* to begin with, you were eliciting. And such incited answers are devised to be utterly forgettable, an obligatory higher twaddle."

Daydream: an interviewer from said global publication arrives, GPS-directed, at my house and demands to know: "What is the meaning of it all?" Me: "Oh, come off it."

Intellectuals: There are ants busy building anthills and anteaters happily eating them up and (I don't actually know if they do this) trampling over the anthills. What a blessing not to live in a center of "vibrant intellectual activity," but in a community of learning, beavering on.

Glorious parochialism: Annapolis trumps New York.

Professors profess (tell what's what), editors edit (change "he" to "she"), managers manage (update procedures), inventors innovate (increase speed). If they must, they must, but why must I applaud?

21 INTEREST

As music is the food of love, so interest is the sustenance of work.

A sign that the world is well-supervised after all: Solidity is, in the long run, more charming than charm. And engaged interest is irresistible. Not vagrant smartness.

"He has wrong-headed convictions, and he hasn't even the courage of those." Then shouldn't we shout hurrah?

Actually, there's some safety even in the fact that people often hold on to egregious misapprehensions with clenched rigidity but without living interest. Break-out is feasible.

Interest is the agar, the growing medium, for talk, friendship, action. And yet, as gourmands abstain from feeding to sharpen the appetite and Protestants defer gratifications to further their enterprises,* shouldn't we sometimes damp interest, withdraw from being among (*inter-esse*), and make a space for untethered felicity instead? It's not for long, anyhow: "Enough! No more: / 'Tis not so sweet now as it was before."†

* Max Weber's "Protestant ethic."
† *Twelfth Night.*

There's a kind of laziness that evinces itself in business, what Pascal calls diversion: Anything rather than think.

Respectful admiration lassoes its object without throwing it—a shameful half-way effect in catching a cow, according to my cowboy friend Randy, but, in my pretty far-fetched metaphor, better than the whole. As the Greeks said (I think; if not, they ought to have): *to hemisu pote kreitton tou holou*, "the half is sometimes better than the whole."

Staring: appalled prurience. Gazing: loving interest.

Nothing gets done without will-power? "Don't be being funny." (Moscow telephone operator's reply to a cheeky Johnny—now deceased—who called the Kremlin from our coffeeshop and asked to speak to Khrushchev). What gets things done is *interest*—object-focused love, or better, large desire pin-pointed to the occasion.

Learning is of the lovable. This is an explanatory expansion of the sentence "Learning is of the learnable," in which "the learnable," called by philosophers the "formal object," tells what kind of thing is fit to activate the action of learning. As the original dictum is not an innocent analytic (meaning redundant) proposition, so the exegesis is not obvious; people might object that you can learn things that are ugly and repulsive. To be sure, you can become acquainted with them, be trained to deal with them. But I think that the learnable really is, *ipso facto*, the lovable, meaning that learning embraces whatever it takes up and acts on it by a clasp of regard: That's what I call *interest*. So if you are really to learn vexatious matter—something beyond facing and mastering it—you'll have to allow it to captivate you, as being in its negating way darkly beautiful and grandly revelatory (as, for example, Milton's horrific hell is). But it may be a corrupting sophism to solve the question of learning's formal object by claiming that *everything* can be seen in the purifying light of love, that everything is transmuted by the alchemy of interest. Rather the eminently learnable really is, in itself, lovable. So the most innocently beautiful of subjects—innocent, not innocuous—is called quite simply *mathematics*, Greek for "learnables."

PERPLEXITIES

Came recently on this passage in Mann's *Doktor Faustus*:

> "Do you consider love to be the strongest affect?" [*Leverkühn*] asked.
> "Do you know a stronger one?" [*Zeitblom*]
> "Yes, interest."
> "By that you probably understand a love from which animalistic warmth has been eliminated?"
> "Let's agree to that definition!," he laughed. "Good night."

Perplexity One: I must have first read this over a half century ago. Was it so germane to my nature, did I assimilate it so completely as to think, on this late re-reading, that I, not Leverkühn, answered Zeitblom? And was

I practicing my own pro-plagiarism policy?—the one I preach to myself in behalf of our students: When I come on my own thoughts, lifted by a student from one of my screeds all but verbatim, I should rejoice—it's a bit of teacher's triumph.* Anyhow, shouldn't there come a moment when the patent on basic truths has lapsed, and so the obligation to reference ideas is time-expired, even in the adult world? Where's the line between plagiarizing and absorbing?

Perplexity Two: But hold it. Leverkühn's elevation of interest (my most admired affect) is, after all, alien to me. Love shouldn't be specified as animalistic, and interest should not be qualified as frigid. If the latter is devoid of anything, it's not warmth but possessiveness. Interest is unpossessively ardent love. Then, where's the line between absorbing and purloining?

General afterthought: Ironic scruple, supercilious distance, doesn't do it. The "buts," "howevers," "on-the-other-hands" of doublethink and doubletalk are precisely marks of interest, of *interesse*, "being among," of intimacy-ready inclusivity rather than withdrawal-prone exclusivity. Thomas Mann is, page by exhaustive page, the most unfailingly attention-holding writer I know, especially in his own German, but in his ironic distance he lacks the great grace of the Anglo-Saxons and the Russians: unabashedly naïve love. And so he is, somehow, not so interesting—where "somehow" is not hand-waving but defining of my terminal ambivalence.

*At least with our students, of whom the most Program-engaged tend also to be the most influence-resistant.

Two causes of rebellion and war: inexpressiveness and unoccupied time: gaggedness and boredom.—Perhaps *the* causes?*

* Found belatedly: Aristotle on the dangers of uneducated leisure (*Politics* VII).

Eventually, to do justice to the one subject you care about you have to be interested in many. But not at first: monomania makes a good launch into learning.

Over and over: there's no debility in supposed-to-be learners like lack of interest. It's a wickedly therapy-averse case: the more incantations you sing to bring the corpse of thereness to life, the deader its sleep. So finally do what fits the case, although it skews the aim: *threaten*, in the— slim—hope that a kick-start by the alien motive of fear will occasion a wake-up in the germane mode of desire.

Once more: these are my watchwords: *Respect*—appreciative "looking at," and *interest*—companionate "being among"—etymology at its most satisfying.*

* Usage is less felicitous. Like everything worthy, these words have a darker side: "respect to person" can mean "squinting unfairly at status." "Having an interest in" can mean "being advantage-seekingly involved"; the disclaiming term is "disinterested," "free from ulterior motive"—which, in turn, is often misused for "uninterested." I take this solecism to betoken that the original positive meaning, so valued by me, is still the potent one.

22   INTROSPECTION

Do I want an accurate picture of my aspect to others? Since when I imagine it, I shudder, I conclude that I can really do without it. In fact, though generally without inhibition in these scribbles, I cringe at driving my pencil (for that's what I use, a nice, plastic, wood-look-alike screw pencil, enough at hand for the last decade) along the descriptive words that capture my externalities. Last year's commencement provided the parameter-experience, a nice duality. Introduction to first family: "This is Ms. Brann, the embodiment of the Program." Second family: "This is Ms. Brann, our mascot." (*Nota bene*, our big neighbor, the Naval Academy has for its mascot an old billy goat.)

Public derogation of tradition, in its self-certainty, is risibly arrogant. And yet, isn't that just what we joyfully do in self-communing—know for sure how whatever is, might be, were our advice but heeded, better?

Provisional clarity is most likely to come to the permanently boggled mind.

A mind (like mine) that is crossed by practically everything in the course of a week misses the point shamefully at times. So watch out! But for what?

I recommend this eerie experience of self-alienation: Look in the mirror at your face—not your grooming—and wonder: why is *this* me, this inadequately small frontage to the vast territories of the soul? What a blessing that its aspects, front and behind, have never been seen directly by me!

Don't I know how much conceit and deceit there is in all I say? But let's be reasonable. If I weren't in it, why would I speak at all, and if I prefaced all I said with proper disclaimers about its truth-reach, how would I ever begin? If what I or anyone says exceeds self-promotion or advances into truth even by a millimeter, why engage in self-flagellation about being human?

Moments of heart-stopping alienation: this hand, here, now, wielding an eraser-topped pencil. Really mine? This face, here, now in the bathroom mirror. Why me?

Everything should be small-scale around me except my scope of interest.

Is she opaque or am I obtuse?

When you've settled with yourself, then you're open for business, because your energies are fired up to be invested in otherness, always the more interesting direction.

Of course I don't know how others talk to themselves, but I can't imagine that it's in the sloppy, formulaic colloquialism of the social world; I imagine that they address their internal *alter ego* with the supple formality evoked by respectful intimacy. Here's the practical effect of this surmise when helping students with their writing: "How did you put it to yourself, before you squashed it flat to be put on paper (or screen)?"

Meditation, 12:27 AM, Thurs, Dec 2, 2010, after Seminar
ON BEING RICH (BY MY LIGHTS)

Funny; the things one has in fact thought of—what hasn't one (stupid, this pretense of impersonal everybody-ness, when I mean me, myself, I)—what hasn't passed over my mind that I nonetheless continue to think un-thinkable? In an odd moment I transit into a world not native to me: my money, surviving me. How much is it? I have no idea, since I listen to my very communicative investment advisors, face alert with desirous intelligence and an intellect dulled with woolly incomprehension. (Actually I *know* finance is fascinating, I just don't *believe* it; the same with my medical reports. From the former I want safe increase, from the latter rapid relief.) Any-how, I'm a Donor, sitting at a fancy lunch between my fi-nancial counselor and my beneficiary (Vice President for Advancement—comical title if heard with wicked inno-cence).* So it turns out I'm rich, in a small way—rich from just sitting on it and investing no energy in spend-ing it—and so I'm a patron sitting between two profes-sionals—a somebody.

Here's a thought with absolutely no resonance: I could spend it, say, in travel, buying stuff. Aye, there's the rub: Go where? Buy what? At the moment, I'm in the blessed state in which if I go anywhere I'm invited, and mostly paid for. As for buying stuff, every item is a liability. I never wear my nice clothes for fear of deterioration, and I don't pick up attractive objects for worry they'll turn into clutter. Moreover, I know well: Every dollar spent draws another after it; even books: Buy a book, need a bookcase. I wasn't made for managing riches but for clearing the decks so that reality can eventuate: talking, learning, bantering, studying, being with old friends who are both comically and poignantly themselves, teaching lovable kinds who are both uniquely themselves and generically alike (a true description)—and the occasional illuminations of having thought something out.

What about being a somebody in the World? Well, I'm a big (plump) frog in a very little pond and croak lustily when called upon. How'd that happen? Longevity and virtues tailored to the community: appreciative collegiality, conversational readiness, home-grown learning, indefeasible amateurism, only occasionally flagging enthusiasm for our work—and for the institution a mixture of recalcitrance and loyalty that keeps sentiment from becoming sentimentality. Beyond that, a life whose privacies breed the matter for public discourse.

But all that is not being Somebody, a category of worldly esteem in which I appear comical to myself. Having money looks seriously good on some people, say our board members, like being hung about with bells and whistles; it wouldn't on me, even if I were in their league. Here's *my* source of pride: I'm a member of a real community of learning, a true communism, in which the most able give all they can and the least take what they need, a communion of somewhat unequal equals (in different respects), giving and taking with mutual gratitude. The moving principle is ardent *interest* (once more, my favorite word: "being among"), which is careful love, meaning an affect more inclined to discreet reverence than clamoring closeness. That's my realm—and my colleagues'—and relative obscurity is its protective mantle. Happily, I'm congenitally obscure.

*As I may, since J.A. does somewhere (in the novels or letters?): "Rears and Vices"—speaking of admirals.

AFTERTHOUGHT *(4:30 AM)*

The accumulation of—moderate—wealth which took place, so to speak, behind my back, without my lifting a finger beyond signing an occasional paper, seems like sheer magic, a sort of sin-less usury, unearned gain, cheerfully received.

Did I ever deprive myself, practice Jewish financial acumen, Protestant deferred gratification? Never. I just didn't much want the stuff and its burdens. Less nobly put: I thought and felt *small scale* in matters of so-called lifestyle. Behind that (call it expense-philistinism) is a childhood obsession (call it an ethico-esthetic sensibility) for keeping my immediate sphere under control, eradicate idle duplications and opaque accumulations (a propensity never extended to other people's messes—I can say that for myself).

Not applicable to books. For other gear, it's one item in, one item out, but ever since my traveling book-box came home to roost, it's been addition, addition. None goes out: I'd rather buy a book for a friend than lend mine. (The bad books can stay, but have to lie on their sides, stacked way on top of their case; once an acquaintance gave me a book of hard pornography of his own inditing. I dropped it into a trash can in Grand Central

Station: witless bawd!) Giving away isn't in it: The day after, that's the one I'll want.

The ethical part of this is that there've got to be some clear surfaces for configuring in space what is handy to the spirit. The esthetic part is that clutter prevents comeliness; living in an unperspicuous mess degrades one's style. The sensibility part tells me that as human sentimentality is like putrid sentiment, so thing-attachments is like petrified affection. But then my pictures and mementoes, all home-made or given me, aren't "things."

Go back to bed. Well, a mug of hot chocolate (sugarless) first.

Introspection is really our best recourse for self-knowledge, insofar as the world is more often a mirror than an interpreter. But Hegel shows that other selves are indeed needed to elicit the full experience of self-consciousness. I waffle. My appearance doesn't seem to me to be much in sync with my being, though my kindly friends and my reluctant self have worked on it long enough. What when I'm a crumbling corpse and some curious body stumbles on this? Will I finally *be* rather than appear? Will I have succeeded in being a bona fide self? *No*, because it will turn out that appearance is the *frontage* of our being, and when that's fallen away, we—I mean all the testimonies we leave of ourselves—are like a house after a bombing: all the rooms open to view but no life left in them.

Moral: Don't imagine you can outlive yourself in your mere works. They'd better have a life of their own.

My ideal: subtle mind, plain ways.

23   KOOKINESS

The art of being interesting excludes overt eccentricity—but derives from inner kookiness.

Self-declared New Yorkers—women especially—are *weird*, blissed out on agony, discretionarily ugly, implausibly sophisticated, especially from the waist down (knee-high boots in 90°)—and the males in cowboy boots. Twenty-four hours and I suffer from terminal sensory overload. But they wouldn't live anywhere else, or better, think there *is* nowhere else. Go figure.

First there were boor-scientists, then emulating boor-humanists, best-selling boor-theologians, much-published boor-philosophers, and—who'd have believed it of vegetarians—even boor-buddhists: lusty know-nothingism.

Great men's kookiness and kinkiness (*re* Newton's papers): Why expend wonder on it, when people perfectly rational-seeming in an ordinary way also have great reserves of pure kook in them (I should know). Much of what is regarded as intellectually kinky is just a tactlessly recalcitrant insistence on getting the meaning out of what people too sane for their own good overlook as evanescently obvious.

Admirable. Outside: distinction without eccentricity. Inside: aberration without pathology.

Anyone who just is what he is, is *ipso facto*, appealing/annoying in equal parts—appealing for the naiveté, annoying for the same.

"I want to be alone"—great; a collateral relief for the world.

People announce bizarre opinions; where do they get them? By applying current platitudes to eccentric notions. Today an elderly lady in my class bids me live in the twenty-first century. How can one "live in" a century and why would she want me to move into a dangerous neighborhood? Day before, a retired lawyer, once great in his line, tells me (news of the week) that you gather information (his source is ever open before him), and then you make up your mind. What an odd notion! Surely the sane order (or, in any case, the inevitable one) is: desire, decide, develop the rationale, only then trawl the tide of fact for support. And when you just can't hook the catch you're fishing for, give up citing your information.

Sure, facts figure in judgment calls, but before that it's a judgment call whether facts are to figure. Sometimes "Against all odds" trumps all facts, especially the pertinent ones. Example, from the deaning years, psychiatrist's advice: "She's on the brink of a breakdown; send her home." What? Into the arms of its precipitators? I was anxious, but we both lucked out.

Here's what "being secure" means: an absolute conviction that *I'm* the measure of normality. Otherwise put: *my* kookiness is not an aberrancy but human nature detailing itself.

24 LOVE

Here's a point of pride: Lovability (almost) never fails to raise the proper response in me.

A touch of evil is no impediment to love but a taint of baseness is. Parse this who can.

In matters of love *non* takes precedence over *sic*, because admission to intimacy is the most discriminating *gift* in our bestowal. The religion that commands universal love as a *duty* can't mean *that* Love. Of course not. Love, *Eros*, is a pagan god; *agape* pales before him.

The Christian Bible fascinates me in part because I don't know what these apostles and disciples are talking about: It's so intense and yet so un-lusty.

Blind love: defects occulted, for prostration's sake. Seeing love: flaws noted, for pity's sake.

Love is to lust as diffusion is to contraction: the former is slow-spreading, long-breathed, aspectful, the latter urgent, abrupt, blind—probably a woman's view.

Love occasioned : admiring
Love unconditional : parental
Love possessive : erotic
Love demanding : needy

and their interweaving.

True Love, they say, is unconditional. How can it be true if it's not for cause? Nothing is lovelier than love for cause. Isn't the poetry of love largely the noting of causes?

What is more unreasonable than to feel gratitude for gratuitous gifts, like love? Yet what is more graceless than *not* to feel it?

For antiquity, pity foreclosed love, for Christianity it forwards it—a candid versus a sentimental sensibility.

It's not uncommon, maybe more among men than women, to fear, even in ardent love, a loss of freedom, to shrink from the need for accommodation in small things. (Think of Pierre Bezukhov's surprise at the possessive demands made by Natasha, and as in the novel, so in life.) These curtailments of little liberties are finally willingly accepted in return for delights and comforts secured. What's rare is the unwillingness to give up large freedom, a heroic life, an exposed eminence (in one's own estimation), to forgo the bracing winds that blow through a solitary life.

Admiration for what you do, love for who you are.

Perhaps parental love is unconditional, perhaps God's love. But all the other loves, even (perhaps especially) love of country, are for cause. Intimate love (surely especially) is *sustained* by goodness, even if it's first *incited* by grace, which, although a gift and not a virtue, is, nonetheless, itself a cause. Such love is, to be sure, not quite articulable, precisely because it is too particular for expression in words and, by the same token, it's anything but indeterminate. And when it goes, cause—grace or goodness—being gone, what remains is loyalty, except for this bedevilment: once really in love, always in love. So maybe it's unconditional, after all?

Only mothers have love enough to forgo possession. The Levite's wife who put Moses among the cattails by the riverbank and the harlot before Solomon who gave up her son rather than see him cut in two are only the oldest examples. So the notion that mere lovers want the beloveds' happiness enough to give up their presence to obtain it for them—that's unreal. They'd rather know them in Hades than out of reach on earth; in fact, inexistence is a comfort to rejected lovers. That's romantic love; everything to do with romanticism plays with death.

Hearts get broken, and some people even die of it. But the killer is not the breaker, who, to be sure, bears some blame, but the victim who, when all is reckoned up, has chosen to commit a probably punitive suicide. As for the sorry survivor: He who weeps last, weeps best, after all.

If you bestow love on the billions as your brothers, you probably haven't much left for your own. But seriously, what effective fellow-feeling is owed to distant and unknown humanity? Practical solution: for those near and dear, personal and practical care; for those far away occasional contributions to professional surrogates.*

*Irresistible: Dignified alien lands on earth, bringing his planet's Book, entitled *To Serve Man*. Eager do-gooding earthling takes off for this philanthropic star, too soon to learn what kind of book it is: the culinary kind. (Told me by my friend and translation-buddy Peter; from a *Twilight Zone* episode. Actually adapted from C.S. Lewis, *Narnia* 4, *The Silver Chair*, "Something Worth Knowing"; and that was told me by my other translation-buddy, Eric Salem.)

A: "I came to ask for your forgiveness for what I said." B (spoken): "No forgiveness needed; you did me no wrong." (Unspoken): "You did show me that what we are to each other is not the same." Not a wrong, but worse.

None of this is unexceptionally true, which means it's not a generic mark. But for young males it seems to be almost impossible not to be erotically aroused by whomever; for young women (at least old style; they still exist) it's almost equally hard to be so casually attracted, and actually falling in love is a rare, almost miraculous and often once and for all event—a laborious product of the imagination with sex as a by-product. The sexualization of very young women is a great loss to fantasy life and—who knows?—may spell, for a few centuries, the end of grand novel-writing except in the historical genre.

Calibrated inattention, calculated unavailability, selective forgetfulness—the evasive maneuvers of a heart unready to hurt and determined to cast loose. Recognize it!

Some people grow more lovable the longer they're dead.

Who really understands what's behind the absolute divide between casual and intimate touch—the one bestowed in a spirit of fairly indiscriminate friendliness, the other terminally discriminating? There's a bit both of vulgar familiarity and of warm humanity in the embracings of Christianity and its offshoot, democracy, with their all-hugging *agape*. Antique *Eros*, then and now, is exclusive—the ultimate aristocracy of the flesh.

Who needs/wants to love humanity when there are people around!

Charity is an effort or an expenditure and naturally requires gratitude, often not readily forthcoming. Love is no effort at all and costs nothing and so deserves no gratitude, but often elicits it. Life isn't fair, "they"—rightly—say. In fact it's amazing how often "they" are right.

The autoeroticism of object-devotion—unlike fellow humans the thing will never resent the importunities and assaults of the lover and may, in course, surrender. But also, unlike humans, it cannot give comfort in need; in fact it denies itself to the mendicant suitor. So the love is asymmetrical and the lover solitary: Newton. But the reward is high in insight and mastery.

More accurately: the impassioned connoisseur of a non-human object, be it of beauty or of truth, projects his own love outward while extracting, evolving, the object's love toward himself. Thus he hosts both his own love for the thing and its reciprocal possession of him. (Why "he"?)

How and when to gauge the depth of an attachment? "At bottom," "when all is said and done," "at the right moment," "over the years"?

Is loving in one's power? Maybe, but it's not will-power.

Love begins in delight and evolves into care; whether that's just dull duty depends on a skill learned in tending an old-fashioned stove: how to bank the fire so that a flame will again shoot up when the time comes. The embers of duty can shelter the glow of delight.

Labors of love work inversely to labors of kindness. The latter should be *accepted* with gratitude for the service opportunely rendered, whereas the former will be *extended* with gratitude for the gift being willingly received.

Sexual intimacy: In the young years of the sexual revolution casual "relationships" were an exhilarating transgression. Now it's like getting your driver's license, people are surprised that you haven't yet taken the test. The relief from pressure and the increase in pleasure is probably quite valuable, but there is a loss of something invaluable: tension. Actually it's a loss-leader: ease now, anxiety later.

"Let's start all over, new beginning." "Well, then, let's," though we both know it'll all go downhill again before long. But that's what makes it OK: Then we can't blame ourselves for forcing novelties on an emotional world dying to stay the same.

Can anyone want to be loved by someone they don't love? Served, helped, protected, yes; these are debts gladly paid in gratitude. But loved? Unreturnable love is a haunting incubus. But to shrug it off, or even glory in it, is plain contemptible.

Plato's *Philebus* is *the* text on the perversity of that desire which is also a need: It hurts before having and ceases upon getting, so its pleasure is passing brief. But Thomas speaks of *fruitio*, the "enjoyment," of what was desired, of wanting *while* having.* That's bliss: once having desired and obtained, still wanting—for good. Perhaps then the key is in distinguishing need from want. Needing is assuaged, wanting is sustained by fulfillment.

* *Summa*, "Treatise on the Passions."

Why does a cool, firm hand convey the deepest warmth? —a question not about physical palpitation but psychic touch.

Well, of course, there comes a time when the acute delight elicited by that sole wonder of the world is dimmed by continual presence. But by then the habit of love has become so ingrained that it's chronic.—And again, of course, there are moments of glistening renewal. And I'm not talking only of human objects of love.

How can so light a thing as a mere touch release such large commotions? Not in proportion to the act but the actor.

Love is always arousal, but with different addresses: groin, bowels, midriff, chest, heart, and yes, head. And it always has an object, but of various sorts: plant, animal, child, man, woman, *objet d'art*, land, divinity, and yes, itself. If each object can address every venue, that makes fifty-four distinct loves, and I haven't remotely got them all. Moreover, each love can surely command at least one epic, lyric, tragedy, novel, or essay, but probably multitudes, and each work in each genre can tell of any combination of love-types. And that all the above has been and is and will be going on: deliciously horrible thought!

A test of love is whether it survives through somatic variations, especially slight ones. Someone "in love" can be put off by a pimple, for in such love the fastidious devil *is* in the singular details. It is fixated, thus brittle; sentimental, thus delicate; passionate, thus demanding; surface-bound, thus skating. That's the narrow particularity of appearance-bound *love*. *Lust*, on the other hand, the indiscriminating closure with the flesh, is unaffected by somatic subtleties; it's less soulful but more robust. And finally there is the soul's love, which is large, loyal, and physically forgiving, and can survive even the discontinuities of appearance wreaked by distance and time.

A too-exquisite sensibility and a too-primitive lust equally bypass Eros. Both the scholasticism of feelings by which they too finely discriminate themselves into subtle categories and the analphabetism by which passion despoils itself of every literary resonance are outside the god's domain; he is at once affectively focused and poetically variegated.

Since romantic love is essentially acutely, even pathologically, concentrated attention, the object is a congelation of highly specific qualities—and that makes for fragility: the toss of the head, the beam in the eye, the set of the chin, all may one dull day fail to move. Can the stable excellences of the soul substitute? Well, the poignancy of looks is distributed into an infinite variety of enchanted somatic detail, which, unless the object is Cleopatra-like, familiarity can certainly stale,* while the goodness of the soul, more chary of appearance, is safely withdrawn behind the beguiling facade. But if you've learned to read even the de-magicked body for its soul, that's no longer "in love" but love—if the soul so deciphered still invites it.

*Antony and Cleopatra: "Age cannot wither, nor custom stale / Her infinite variety."

Opposite reflections of love: "The flow of beauty goes back to the boy from the eyes of the lover."* "I saw Othello's visage in his mind . . ."† The boy sees *himself* projected from his lover's eye; it's a *self-reflected relation*. His beauty, which is literally an image in his beholder's eye, its "pupil,"‡ is sent back to him, and he knows himself as being lovable. That's being a *beloved*. But the woman, in a startling reversal of the commonplace that the soul appears in the face, sees the man's countenance within his soul: she enters his soul and loves him from the inside out, consecrates her soul "to his Honours and his valiant parts," which bear his visage. It's the very essence of *other-focused love*, of love that passes *within the other*, even there finding his face. That's being a *lover*.

*Phaedrus.

Conditional love's stages: amazed admiration at first sight, specified admiration from closer in, captivated admiration for good; that's the progressive attraction which bears the soul's stamp of approval: love that advances with friendship.

For acts of love, gratitude is gratuitous—acceptance says it all. (Accepting is not *mere* taking, as in "taking for granted.")

Desire self-destructs, love self-sustains in achievement.

Once again: The god-statue, object of adoration and non-interactive delight (so unlike Donne's ecstatic union: "Our eye-beams twisted and did thread / Our eyes upon one double string")—the self-moving statue that we watch, wanting nothing but to *be there*, to observe the gracious distance, engagedly disengaged, unencumbered by the leash of longing, to watch a divinity whose mere being-by-us (so to speak) is our fulfillment.

Then we come to, and ordinary self-ishness with its tit-for-tat requirements, its demand for reciprocity, its expectation of passion-simultaneity. *Inde incipit*, "here it begins": The Relationship. Negotiations of privileges and rights, exacted mutualities and reemerging individualities. The god becomes annoying, in short, has come down to earth. *Inde iterum incipit*, "here it begins once more": Reality.

Hopeless love: That care should emanate from a crowned—but clueless—regent of the heart is about as likely as that a patented aristocrat should evince nobility.

A range of love: from the pinched blind grip of obsession to the visionary panorama of entranced reflection, and in the middle that defined, particular personal love which is specific to us humans—whose cause is *at once* inarticulately singular and epically cosmic.

Love in old age: hands-off protectiveness and similar contradictions-in-terms.

One way to experience love: as terminal agreeableness.

Some love with discerning ardor, some with simple-minded stolidity, some with . . . I'm falling into the Barrett Browning mode, Eros quantified.*

* "How do I love thee? Let me count the ways."

A mundane image of one afflicted with an unreciprocated love: an overstocked merchant whose most highly prized goods are completely devalued and cannot even be given away.

In love, delight and comfort are quite separable, and which dominates is of consequence. If comfort is an unforced fall-out of the sheer pleasure of being in the other's presence, all's well. But let the need for solace outweigh the sense of gladness, and the attachment tips into dependence—if occasionally, fine; if habitually, not so good.

When love is withdrawn there is a double loss—the deep desolation that follows on the revelation, and the simultaneous privation of the one and only source of comfort.

In the early years, suppressed sexual attraction, later on controlled particular liking—these are, if truth be told, pretty nearly *the* teacher's talent—not a virtue but a *proficiency*. It's the affective continuo to the responsive descant of intellectual engagement with young learners. And it casts loose from gender, being—mostly—directed to the somatic appearance of the *soul*.

Love: fixated attention, being close-held by the attraction of something wonderful. Thinking: fixated attention, being extensively preoccupied by something wonderful. They have similarities (Hegel correctly brings *Andacht*, "devotion" literally "at-thought," together with *Denken*, "thinking.")* Yet objects of thought are hard to get our minds on, and objects of love are hard to get our minds off, and our thinking about love far outruns our love of thinking.

* *Phenomenology.*

Is projected desire more a gift or an imposition, more a favor or an encroachment? It's a question a would-be lover won't want to adjudicate. But of course, declarations of love are at once bestowals and prompts.

Want, *Penia*, is wisely made Eros's mother by Diotima.* Poverty is parent to passion. There is a *universal* matrix of Need from which *specific* want is born, and even the most individual, particular love has its genesis in our generic poverty—as well, according to the priestess, as in resourcefulness, which comes from Provision, *Poros*, the father. Of this patrimony, providedness, Eros is as proud as the rich are of their possessions. As the canny son of universal Need, he is the god of love, of specified desire, but as the endowed child of Provision, he is the lovable god, desire desired. This wisely made myth acknowledges a double mystery: that we fall in love with *this* one, and that we love our having so *fallen*, come what may.

*Plato, *Symposium*.

The understandings of love are so disparate because love bifurcates at the very beginning: happy (or destined to be) and unhappy (or doomed to be). The former is wonderful to experience and a little dull to read of. (It takes a great novelist to make happy domesticity delightful; there *is* that First Epilogue of *War and Peace*.) The happy love is slow, more often feeling than passion, more intimate than public, not in the sense of "no one's business" but simply inarticulable in non-platitudes. The other is a pungent pathology, a devilish possession—distances desperately nonclosable, ultimacies hopelessly unfulfilling, the very stuff of short poems: *Aus meinen grossen Schmerzen mach ich die kleinen Lieder*, "From my great pains I make the little songs,"* and of long novels: "All happy families are alike, each unhappy family is unhappy in its own way."†

*Heinrich Heine.
† Tolstoy, *Anna Karenina*.

Trust and respect are the thoroughbass of love, its steady continuo, but the melody with its grace notes is love's miraculously thematic agreeableness. And the high descant's occasional coming forth—that's the transit to paradise.

What is more searing to a body wanting love than the casual touch of affection? You don't know what wincing is until you've observed (or felt) it.

The ancients called Eros a tyrant, we might say he's a totalitarian. Who ever, under his regime, could understand "Let's cut back some, let's give each other space, I need time to myself" and the whole litany of disengagement? It's all or nothing, and the world as built on love collapses if reduced by a scruple or even a minim. Get out from the tyranny by evolving "in love" into love.—Or fall out of it as you've fallen in, by inadvertence. Can't be done, of course.

Is there passionless, unhungry love such as the theologians claim for heaven's inhabitants? Or is *agape* love that's lost its bite, its *eros*? Entirely toothless love is hard to imagine; even in old age when love is relatively unpossessive, there's some desire—for the love-surrogate properly shown by those three generations behind: affectionate respect. Students are wonderfully gratifying that way.

Delight precedes desire by an unrecoverably light moment, before want, then need, supervenes. The heavenly bodies are better off: the earth's gravity countermands the moon's escape velocity so that they circle each other, mutually attractive, within sight but without contact, for ages. We want to abrogate contemplative delight in favor of possessive collapse. And then it becomes the labor of love to sustain the halcyon instant.

Yes, that's pure glory, it makes one woozy with delight: when a beloved factuality (why not talk straight: an object of love, not necessarily human) with all its inexhaustible observational aspects leaps together momentarily and momentously with the inner scene and its highly specific feeling-effluvium, as do two oppositely charged pieces of foil—when a real body elicits its imaginative setting.

One might say to another: "You've been good to/for me."—Was that just kindness or something more? Now "just" might seem misplaced applied to that virtue, but here it strongly signifies: "I didn't hear what I was longing to hear." To be the object of gratitude is touching, but we'd prefer to be the object of love.

Love can cure many a sickness of the spirit, but it does aggravate pangs of conscience (or guilt feelings, if you go in for that kind of thing).

Admiration derived *from* love is vulnerable and liable to eventual collapse (as is love), but love consequent *on* admiration is solid and reliable in the long run (as is judgment).

The state of impassioned love, heart and soul, leaves nothing over—if it's the real thing, it's one object at a time. But as it closes you to a second love so it opens you to friendships: love and friendship are well paired. The reasons are dual, noble and not-so noble: expansive receptivity and escape valve.

The most poignant emotion: to see a man you love engrossed in devotion to a high cause—the miracle of a rival beyond envy.

Glory: to watch a person to whom one is already bound by intimate love functioning in public, in charge, competent, and authoritative; to see one's own love refracted by the world's admiration, to be privy to the inner genesis of external excellence: Distance *can* magnify.

We're at once a species of one (as each angel is in the heavenly order) and one of a species (as each animal as in the natural taxonomy)—incomparably unique *and* commonly human. And that duplicity is the condition of personal love.

Up close or afar, within full view or on a tangent, in talk or in silence—preserve love-fraught distances. Total closure goes viewless.

> Love seeketh not itself to please,
> . . . .
> Love seeketh only self to please,—

William Blake, "The Clod and the Pebble," found in *Middlemarch*, Chapter 25. Now why do I think more of Eliot for finding it than of Blake for writing it? Not my poet, that's why.

Passion is fluid and fungible until it's focused: then it's unbudgeable.

"Need" is to "want" as a limping iamb (I *need:* ˘ -) is to a running trochee (*I* want: - ˘). "Need" starts with me reduced by a lack, "want" starts with me expansive with desire. Otherwise put: "I need" starts empty and begs for a sufficiency; "I want" starts well-provided and demands abundance. Which tends to win? Wasn't it said: "To him who hath, shall be given"?

If I could describe with precision the difference between the way my possessively demanding, perfectionist attention was riveted on my first bicycle at eight and on my first love at fourteen, I'd be much wiser: I'd know the difference between thing-eros and human-Eros, between intense interest in an object and intense focus on a subject. As it is, I'm comfortably confused.

Love performs this miracle: comfort and excitement at once.

25 MEMOIRS

Years ago three of us went to a costume party: Elliott dressed as Tristan, Beate as Isolde and I, between them, carried a placard "and"—"*das kleine Wörtchen 'und.'*"* I felt *well* labeled—*ampersand*† is my proper middle name.

*Wagner, *Tristan und Isolde*.
† "Ampersand" is the name of the sign that represents "and": &.

Eighty-fifth birthday party at Chris's house. Many evidently heartfelt encomia. Wasn't I in my glory? Of course. But with misgivings, unease. Not because of modesty, of which I haven't a smidgen—though, I hope, a sober assessment of my worth, limitation, and badness. But because I was having to draw overdrafts on my inner savings account—where I bank as smugness-credit the world's obscurity-debit. Now I owe, big-time.

How much sweeter to be serenely sure of having been underestimated than to have to sink through the floor shamed by clueless overpraise.

Respect we deserve to get; adulation we deserve not to get.

Generally my "seat in life," as the Germans say,* is safe enough, but sometimes a demon pulls out this chair, and since it's only figurative I don't crash onto my rear but stay suspended: What am I? Or even more up in the air: What good am I? Dark illuminations, unseated thoughts.

Apropos phrases: A Russian lady, a faculty wife, who had an original relation to English, used this version of "Take a seat." She would invite her guests to "Take place," which we did, happily eventuating at her delectable hospitality. (The same lady would speak of that incomparable story, "Billy the Bud.")—Thus vitiated by the felicitous infelicities of demi-idiomatic English, the demonic pranksters scuttle off.

* *Sitz-im-Leben*: Dilthey? Just for fun, they also speak of *Sitzfleisch*, literally "sit-flesh," meaning "butt," signifying "stick-to-itiveness"; English says it more picturesquely: to revise these scribblings I all but have to "stay glued to my seat." (Ann Martin, who not only saved me from many an error but also filled in many a lacuna, says that the term was originated by a theologian, Hermann Gunkel.)

I never know exactly what to do, but I know pretty much for sure what not to do. Is this what Socrates meant by his *daimon*? So for me, it's always barging ahead on a very wide road very securely lined by a cold ditch on one side and a crackling electric fence on the other.

Will there be retribution for absorbing shamelessly so much good luck?—much of it with a dark side: Millions murdered and America gained, better even than its more consanguine alternative, Israel; feelingless insurrection against good parents and, for my sins, corroboratively favorable outcomes; academic apostasy from a fairly romantic profession, archaeology, and a made-to-measure refuge at my college; but above all, minimal mental suffering, compared to the driven truth-pursuit of those I dub to myself "the agonizing thinkers," from Schopenhauer to Wittgenstein—and unearned occasional breakthroughs.

To my mind there's no contest, at least not as far as my school and my life are concerned, between conserving maintenance—careful preservation including occasional bold reformation, and "creative destruction"—the humanly heedless economist's mantra which requires present suffering for future prosperity. It's carrying Protestant deferred gratification too far when the cohort whose enjoyment is postponed isn't the one to taste the later rewards.

My pride: I'm only intermittently stupid, but then, like a born Jew, *very*. (Judith, fellow Jew, now dead, of herself: "a charging hippo.")

Celebration for me: my Jubilee year at the college (1957–2007). And once again there's evidence that soul and body aren't, *pace* Aristotle, so perfectly at one: soul's cool, somewhat remote, a little—the Germans say *benommen*, "taken over," benumbed, but delighted, exhilarated as well. The body is less serene, breaks out in hives, obligingly not within public view. Once again, the soul shows itself as partite: twanging emotions and cool intellect. So I have a body and a soul, and the soul has a passionate and a thinking part. All this is stuff every freshman has read, but I'm suddenly distracted from the festivities: Why is the ancients' *psychologia* (an account of the soul) more persuasive than our modern *psychology* (a science of the psyche)? Is it because they didn't have their introspections overridden by professional protocols?

People say I must write my memoirs. Well, these are they. Moreover, what I won't say because I take pleasure in not giving it away, or because it's embarrassing (*nota bene*: without being very fascinating), or because it's inarticulable, or because, though it's full of interest to me, it's surely boring to the world, leaves little to report: Nearly sixty years in the right place, a *nunc stans* of threescore that collapses into the day leading up to this present one, with memorable discontinuities recollectable by an occasional prompt; interest- but not incident-laden, the vibrant stasis of daily fulfillment, the brief delight and ready oblivion of an anecdote living itself out; love and loss, learning and misplacing, fighting and giving in— just what makes life coherent is *not* (*pace* literary-theory types who believe that we live narratives) what makes it a story, a plot. For, as Aristotle rightly observes, a story has a beginning and an end and therefore a center. Now the telling of my beginning, live enough in dreams, doesn't engage me much by day. To Americans, particularly some of the young, it might seem mildly remarkable, but to me it's just what I've always known and relived now and then in those fugue states and spontaneous reminiscence-pop-ups that teach us what lurks behind our normalcy. And the telling of the end is out of my power (though in imagination I sometimes pull the Tom Sawyer trick of attending my own memorial and laughing my head off at how presumably veracious speakers saw me or the whoppers they feel it is decent to tell). As for the center, I am, I hope, yet in it. What I've written in this apparent miscellany seems quite coherent to me.—Wasn't it engendered in the same heart, evolved in the same land, inscribed by the same pencil (actually, scores of them)?

On rereading an old writing of mine: I'd like to meet this character; I've got a thing or two to say to her.

If some people were reading my writings for real, they would notice an autobiographical leaning: how eagerly I assert and protect my amateur status. (My one professional book was on Attic Geometric and Protoattic pots, of the later eighth and seventh century B.C.E.).* It's for a bad and a good reason: it exempts me from peer review (it's hard to find people similarly engaged), and it allows me to disport myself in the "naked emperor" domain (who'll cry "The emperor is naked" when there's no crowd to hear?). By the way, I loved being one of the world's few specialists in early Athenian pottery, and flexing my newly achieved competence muscles. But too many pressing questions were proscribed at the excavation's tea table. Gained: unforgettable terminology by the magnificent termagants who ran the Catalogue Room of the Agora Excavations, such as for child urn-burials: "potted brats."

* I managed to subvert even that meticulous labor by dreaming one night that a row of pot-bellied amphorae were dancing all around, while I flitted about frantically to keep them from keeling over and shattering. Actually there was a real-life catalyst: a minor earthquake in Athens, when, sitting in my store-and-work room, I watched the pots march towards me on their

shelves. It stopped before they reached the brink. Twenty-seven centuries in the earth only to be shaken to bits once out of it!

One day, while I was studiously examining one of these old pots, our much-respected director peeked in: "Anything new?" That's archaeology: making novelties of antiquities.

My luck: not to have had more friends than I can keep track of, more honors than I can glory in, more money than I can allocate, and more intellect than helps to see what's what (now and then). But a couple of thousand readers for my (and Paul Dry's) books would be good; I'd do with a few score, the thousands are for him.

Small-gauged natures interpret all help needed and accepted as domination, *especially* if no gratitude is exacted.

The sign of psychic health: never grow tired of sameness *and* welcome otherness.

Rule for pills and life: Whatever too much of won't do you any harm also won't do you much good in due measure.

There's a double shame in discovering belatedly that a fellow human feels disrespect for me: that I evoked it and that I was oblivious to it; the second is harder to swallow.

Human nature: Bumped up into first class; outraged because they're out of my menu choice.

What I would wish to be like: Single of heart and diverse in imagination, focused of purpose and large in scope, firm of opinion and wide in receptivity, steadfast of feeling and manifold in love—that is, beyond my philistine Teutonic self.

People like to tell me—I'm to take it as a compliment—that I haven't changed since they first knew me X decades ago. Here's a huge difference: I'm out of the despising business.

As noted, people keep advising me to write my life. Well, it's been too interesting for anything much to have happened. All this, on these pages, *is* my life. What's more, I'm not a great believer in the current exculpatory dogma concerning the self-serving but unconscious, the cunning but irremediable, skewing of one's own memory. I'd be lying away lustily and cannily were I to fall to telling events. So, as an honest woman, I won't.

Some like to be objects of personal care, some centers of general attention—two kinds of disposition, two limits on happiness.

"Entertainment" is like a medicine with side effects that exacerbate the condition: If taken against the blahs, two hours of calculated inanity ratchet merely dull boredom up to *ennui*, really odious *tedium vitae*.

The art of having models (heroes, if you like) without falling into whole-hog imitation: Choose aspects, preferably invisible ones. Evidence of having gone overboard: gestural mimicry.

A woman's manliness: to take no for an answer, accepting the fact that the addressee of plaints is *ipso facto* unavailable.

What I admire: the largeness to like a lot of people plus the focus to see them for real.

A large spirit is preferable to narrow pedantry, to be sure, but sometimes small piddlings *are* the predicate of expansiveness.

As if that were a practical issue: A little *post-mortem* fame is actually preferable to the *intra-vitam* sort: you're excused from answering your fan mail.

26 MORALS

Likable goodness: not spread so thin by general kindness as to be blunted to particular love.

When folks feel compelled to explain your motives to you, almost always as ulterior, or what's a little worse, as rooted in your—imagine—imperfect nature, know that denial is confirmation and counter-argument is confession. Just smirk inside—besides, they're apt to have a point. So they win: self-condemnation is much less subject to self-exculpation than is outside adjudication.

You read about the virtues of the virtue of moderation, and you remember that, by a convenient disposition of nature, lusty youth and busy maturity is soon followed by time-purified age—and yes, that was the fount of that preachment. And you laugh.

Best not to terminally fix an adverse opinion of a fellow human so as not to end up mired in injustice. Which doesn't mean that, when it's your duty, you shouldn't speak definitively. Ready retraction, however, is a mark of self-confidence—as stuckness is of insecurity.

Sometimes you should apologize even when it's the other one who's in the wrong—for having driven him to it.

CNN anchor concluding an interview with a woman lawyer emoting morally: "Thank you for your outrage." And there's our trouble. It used to be: "You're angry? Well, first cool off, and then we'll talk." How did the vice of temper come to stand in for the virtue of concern?

There are *only* mixed motives, but since the rule is *a potiori fit denominatio*, "the name comes from the stronger," we may call a motive by its predominant constituent, however small its edge. Thus some motives may be called pure after all, having but one name, and the possibility of unstained human goodness is saved. "Sophistical" and "sensible" are sometimes almost indiscriminably mixed up, so call this thought sensible.

I notice that my already brittle faith in the Kantian morality of doing as I ought, *particularly* when it's against my inclination, is further undercut by a certain memory of the moral asceticism of my youth: a temperamental inclination (since worn off) to do my duty even against my inclination, thus frustrating the whole "Metaphysics of Morals" by the convolutions of my private proclivities. But there's this reasonable residue: *Principled morality* acquires too many subtleties for use. Go to *personal ethics*: virtues over rules.

"Staunch" or "dug-in"? How much compromise before I'm compromised? How much constancy before I've turned to concrete? Is this a case for flamboyant intuitivity or creeping ratiocination—both to be found at once in some breasts, such as mine? The Greek political-philosophy types call on prudence; I go for Anglo-Saxon muddling-through. Why? Because one way to keep principles safe is to keep them tacit.

"Nice" is more to be valued than "bright," if Marx is right and a commodity's value is the labor power that went into it.* "Bright" comes by nature and is, if anything, unsuppressable. "Nice" sometimes requires really persistent work, so it has more value—a use-value, if you please, as materialized human effort.

* *Capital.*

Are there moments for us non-Luthers when we must post our theses and say: I can no other? If you were looking forward to the opportunity, you probably shouldn't use it.

How to turn a moral advantage into a human defect: be brutally candid.

A friend, learned in the Jewish Bible, tells me that no human being has the power of forgiveness. That's OK by me; forgiving, a heartfelt pleasure to the forgiver, is at most a relief to the forgiven. Just forget it—forgetting is better than forgiving—except for injustice that has implications for the world. To that the right response is, I think: defang the doer and say to the deed: NEVER AGAIN. Folks repelled by Hebrew harshness should understand: that sentiment vibrates through Israel, from her founding.

I've never figured out how the two maxims in the lobby of Apollo's Temple, "Know Thyself" (*gnothi seauton*) and "Nothing Too Much" (*meden agan*), hang together. If the most ardent proponent of the first, Socrates, were required to fill out a self-assessment form, he would surely be entitled to put N/A in the box for Moderation, since "Nothing too much" can't be a virtue in the pursuit of self-knowledge.* Nonetheless, Socrates isn't one to go overboard. Instead, in his person he obviates excess by being extreme without physical or psychic loss of control. He drinks all night without getting drunk or even sleepy, stands stock still all day and all night without keeling over or needing rest, out-talks, out-thinks, out-dares everyone. "Nothing Too Much" is just "Not Applicable," because nothing *is* too much for so potent a *daimon*.

*The Socratic, non-therapeutic sort: not *self*-knowledge, but self-*knowledge*.

Once again, Apollonian moderation: Is it not an invitation to a continually compromised conscience? Only if you're a constitutional non-pagan, that is, a person of faith with a propensity for purity.

Ascend through these: disdain, ignore, tolerate, respect.

Between pure extremism and muddled moderation it's a no-brainer: the former wreaks irrevocable havoc, the latter just makes a clean-uppable mess.

Among us civilized types, modesty well-governed, says Bacon,* is but an art of ostentation. So too is simplicity, I say, but the art is greater, and naturalness is no different, with the art superlative. Thus cultivatedly simple naturalness is the perfection of the human artifact. It used to be thought the prerogative of a birth-nobility, but it turns up in the American heartland, especially. And it's always a little ostensive, having to do with self-presentation: No civilized being is really modest (but rather open-eyed), or plainly simple (but rather whole-hearted), or truly natural (but rather well-composed).

* "Of Vain-Glory."

Better hide my contempt. It is good manners towards the apparently contemptible object and wise protection for me, the contemptuous subject, who will almost always turn out to be playing the fool.

Praise: Enjoy it to its fullest (or fulsomest) and believe more in the bestowers' niceness than in their veracity.

People want to be like certain people, but they don't want to do what those people do to be like that.

The acme of self-centeredness: continual self-denigration.

Shyness is an official pathology, listed in that baneful *DSM*.* That's merely professional self-serving. Yet the whole complex—intrusive modesty, self-confessed shyness, announced inhibitedness—all that touch-me-not-ism—gives me the willies: the signature of over-wrought self-awareness. Get natural: glow greatly at praise, wilt a little at criticism. And don't talk about yourself in excess of the normally allotted slot—less if feasible.

* *The Diagnostic and Statistical Manual of Mental Disorders.*

Who, having received one of nature's gifts, an advantage that it is, on the one hand, undignified for him to call lucky, is, on the other, so obtuse as to call it deserved?—Unless it be by reason of having long and ardently and very specifically desired it?

Once more: does character breed opinions or do opinions shape character? Surely it's reciprocal: Who I am brings forth what I think, and what I propose to myself as true informs my character.

New problem: These reciprocities, much beloved of indeterminists, just kick the can down the road: Do we have a *substratum*, an "under-lay"? There's certainly enough overlay, all the formations and deformation, accretions and abrasions, of life. Which is us?

Wisdoms, not novel: First think, then do research; smart isn't wise; never insist on "doing *the* right thing" because it's *your* right thing; history is drift, get out of it; futz endlessly, especially for the right word; be like everyone else: yourself; addiction isn't a type of love; when everything changes, nothing can; have fun (happiness, American style), but in moderate quantity—even a tad too much, and it's sheer boredom.

Is luck an achievement? Here feeling and judgment part company. Judgment says "No, because then bad luck would be failure, and that's a mean notion." Yet we all (I think) say "I've been blessed"—and mean it to be heard as "undeservedly"; but since we ascribe the blessing to higher powers, who surely know what they're doing . . .

Celebrity: where multitudes know of you and you know hardly a one of them—an out-of-kilter, asymmetrical, in-human human relation, mutual un-knowing. One is a "personality," a pretend-person, to the many, the many are his "public," a pretend companionship to the one. *Fame* has at least these mitigations: it's mostly post-mortem, and it originates in works rather than in personalities.

There is a world of difference between "total" and "whole": a whole is a harmony of parts, a totality is their suppression: a community vs. a sum. One can qualify "total" by "utter" or "absolute," but not really "whole."

Shyness again, a Johnny-come-lately addition to that book of insurance-covered woes, the *DSM*: in childhood, quite proper; in adolescence, sometimes graceful; in adulthood, cravenly egotistic.

"Insecurity" prevents modesty, because the former is a misjudged surrender to self-involvement, the latter a fair judgment of one's standing *sub specie aeternitatis*—normally low but not debasing.

Don't trust the do-gooding of selfless people, the ones that "get involved" because they have no business of their own to mind. I think that sound doing issues from a solidly centered self who acts under the guidance not of intrusive empathy but of considerate analogy: We're *naturally alike* and probably want similar basics; we're *contingently diverse*, and probably want dissimilar embellishments.

And while I'm at it, don't let anyone trump you in victimhood. Most ethnic Americans are refugees of some sort in some generation and think they've been dealt a hard hand, and to accord any of them, *anyone*, primacy in suffering makes for bad blood; actually that precept runs over the whole human gamut, from mothers to minorities.

Deferred, late-emerging gratitude is more mindful and so more gratifying than the tit-for-tat thanks that close a transaction.

The root of cheer: be an opportunist of misfortune. As they say in Washington, "Never let a good crisis go to waste." Make the most of it: "Let it be," again as they say, "a learning experience." So too with unwelcome duties. You're entitled to put them to use, be it as credit accrued for virtue or of gratitude. And if neither of these happens, enjoy the self-esteem.

Be moderate in moderation; excessive caution issues in impetuous outbreaks because you missed the timely moment. Also, too much foresight tempts the fates:

> But, Mousie, thou art no thy lane,
> In proving foresight may be vain:
> The best laid schemes o' mice an' men
> > Gang aft agley.

"Aft" is weak: not "often" but "mostly"—that's even for the *well*-laid schemes. Getting set for the long run seems often to work, but that's not scheming, it's committing.

We—I—tend to becloud beneficent candor with subsequent apology. Was candor really necessary in the first place? And if it was, why the mitigation of retraction? Either speak or keep silent: *Tertium non valet.*

Go, in a bad mood, into the despising mode, and when you've come out of it, be properly abashed by your own obtuseness.

Being good would be much better than being bright. That's not anti-intellectualism, since goodness requires intelligence.

Reaching beyond one's assigned abilities is undoubtedly a way to fulfillment: "Ah, but a man's reach should exceed his grasp"*—but not if it's the forcible clutch of ambition.

* Browning, "Andrea del Sarto."

Robotic pets for the lonely: Socrates talks of the lie in the soul as most deleterious.* He hadn't heard of the lie in the body.

* *Republic.*

"Assume a virtue if you have it not": Regard correction not as denigration but as attention paid.

Not handsome? It has its charms.
Not very bright? It has its charms.
Not competent? It has its charms.
Not charming? It has its charms.
No character? No way.

Is it that I don't trust others' admiration? No, it's that I don't trust my luck.

It is a matter of self-respect that, if you feel yourself able to run circles around your fellows, you abstain. Besides: maybe you really couldn't. Or maybe it impugns your gravity to run in circles.

Public praise: gratefully received, properly discounted.

"Health is the reward for virtuous living": Heavens, no: health is the condition that facilitates virtue—and so devalues it.

"Let right be done"*—a stern command to be obeyed. "Do the right thing"—a self-righteous imposition to be resisted.

* *The Winslow Boy* (Mamet, 1999).

Plato's enigmatic wisdom from the Myth of Er (*Republic* X): Our lives shape us *and* we choose them.

Modesty$_1$: shyness, a grace in the young, a vice in the mature, where it's too much concentration on the self and its privacies, and reserve morphs into feyness. Adult bashfulness has an only occasional, fleeting charm—in others.

Modesty$_2$: a proper sense of my own vanishing importance *sub specie aeternitatis* with a proportionate self-respect *sub specie saeculorum*.

Modesty$_3$: a comportment that prudence and policy enjoin.

Modesty$_4$: the sense of awe, buffered by delight, before the wonder of greatness, shot through with the pride of participation by reason of receptivity.

Gratitude: a generous duty for generous souls to give and to receive. But for the giver there is the slight residue of an obligation exceeding mere thanks, and for the receiver the slightly chilling sense of being liked not for what one is but for how one was useful.

When *apparently* large troubles of your own forestall little humanities for others, you're on the brink of perdition. Oddly, *really* big grief brings distance from those small concerns and finds relief in maintaining the civilized courtesies. "Grace under pressure," humanity in devastation—it's how one should be.

Most motion is commotion. Quiet down and let Aristotle's vibrant stasis (*energeia*) eventuate.

When caught committing brilliance, quickly beg the gods' pardon.—It was but a flash in the pan.

27   MUSIC

A music is playing, a person is present, a scene comes forth: significance is in the air. In the air? No, in the music, person, scene. Trace it, and say it, hold it. Why have perceptions if you're going to let them dissipate before you've fully, *precisely*, apprehended them? Full awareness has two phases: experience and articulation. Who wants a soul that's a lumber-room of never unpacked gifts?

My personal revelation is musical, although (or perhaps because) I'm unmusical, ungifted. (Professional musicians are fixated mostly on intra-musical meaning.) I'm captivated, enthralled by devotional music (not, of course, by those flabby nineteenth century Episcopalian hymns) and correspondingly repelled by recreational music. Through high music there is access to the artful government of the world; it details the heavenly offices. Intermittent admission to these realms erects the soul. It makes me better than myself and more blest than I deserve.

The mystery of pure music: It melds formless affect and wordless meaning into acutely specific significance.

The Christ of Bach's *St. John Passion*, "the hero from Judea," the victim as conqueror, is deeply alien to me, almost repulsive; it has deleterious contemporary resonances. In sober truth victims are, *ipso facto*, diminished, and in real life victimhood is a real liability. A hero is the master, not the victim, of his suffering, I think. I'll take David over Jesus, psalms over parables.—But the music, those world-undulations under *Herr* and *Herrscher*! It's rare that word and sound don't jibe in Bach's compositions—and so much the more food for thought.

"The Art of the Fugue": Twenty-three times the same armature, each differently the same—way beyond my meager musical means to discern. In the last three, Bach or the performers switch from cembalos to clavichords, and they go at it like two heavenly hens clucking away or like the plucking of heartstrings or like the sensualizations of a philosophical colloquy—those plangent sonorities and that sedate tread: the most soberly ecstatic music I know, celestial twanging.

Again, the *Art of the Fugue* on two clavichords: the centered plangency of Paradise, where passionless ardor is said to be the style of love. This music is my soul-mate (not a word previously in my sentiment-dictionary)— if it eventuated as a human being, I think I'd evanesce with joy.

We have to pay the proper dues to our brain, which undoubtedly *governs* much of our secular consciousness, though it only *subserves* our atemporal soul. My proper due is a morning cup of coffee. I pity people who started themselves on stronger stuff way back. "Artificial paradises" are satanic: the stimulation of the central exchange of our somatic humanity, the brain, to achieve psychic excitation is a Faustian soul-sale.

Question to myself: what of music? Why is that addiction—or my need-like love of human works of art—a virtue of which I am, truth be told, actually proud? As so often, the answer, if any, has got to be ultimately theological.

This life of mine with Bach is surely an essentially unmusical, even barbarous habit. And yet, for all that, perhaps more life-supporting than would be a keener, more knowledgeable, more actively attentive listening. Anyhow, mine.

A liberal education (rightly understood) can make you better, but it takes a long time. Bach can do it now. He thought that a musician's task was "to make a well-sounding harmony to the honor of God and the permissible delectation of the soul."* Such music (when really heard) is an aural ethics.

* Quoted from Christian Wolff, *Johann Sebastian Bach: The Learned Musician*, pp. 308–309. On these pages Wolff points out that Bach was, heart and soul, a teacher not only *of* music but also *through* music. When this scholar talked to us about the *Magic Flute*, I was dying to ask him if many of Mozart's operas meet Bach's criterion of "permissible delectation." I forbore.

Bach makes you better than you'd be on your own. For example: A brief burst of chorus to put the soul on alert: *Es ist ein trotzig und verzagt Ding um aller Menschen*

*Hertze.** Don't I know about a defiant and timid heart! But the music says: compose the rift and find a tempered courage.

*Cantata 176, loosely based on *Jeremiah* 17, 9: "There is a defiant and timid something about all human beings' heart."

"If music be the food of love . . ."*—probably it is. But certainly the converse is the case: love is the source of music. More than of everything else? Yes, most of all of music, because love is the most sweepingly universal of affects and music the most minutely specific of arts, and general affect seeks to particularize itself, to realize itself in sensuous concreteness, form-giving specificity. So I imagine that, as an attachment is a particularization of Desire, so its oral effect is a piece of Music: love imaged with exactitude.

* *Twelfth Night.*

The mystery of music: Bach Cantata 21, *Ich hatte viel Bekümmernis*, "I had much anxious sorrow": ravishingly beautiful, upliftingly joyful—and yet it means what it says. I can't make it out.

A CD of the Augsburger *Domsingknaben* (rebranded, or better, rebaptized—used to be *Domspatzen*, I think): the German songs of my childhood, every note familiar. Talk about conflicted! I think of the murderous sentimentality that is not incompatible with this music, *and* I see my happy nursery and hear one root of my musical sensibility. Luckily, there was a countervailing influence, later: *Hava Nashira!*, the song book of the Zionist youth movement. And all along, and beyond all ethnicity, Beethoven out of my parents' domed victrola—for adolescence, and Bach out of our gothic-latticed radio—for life. And when finally my soul is disembodied, this is how I hope it will look: *BWV* 1060, third movement, allegro.*

* *Concerto in C minor*, for Two Harpsichords (*BWV*: *Bach-Werke-Verzeichnis*); runner-up: *BWV* 1062, same key, instrumentation, movement, allegro assai.

Once more, *BWV* 1060, that piece of music which seems to me an audible version, a tonal simulacrum of myself before the Fall: 222 seconds of pure joy. For those three and two-thirds minutes, who needs a next world? Or rather, who could think Paradise impossible?

The god Pan ("All") is everywhere. Herodotus tells how Phillipides, the marathon runner, meets Pan in Arcadia. Ratty meets him as a piper and protector of lost baby otters in the U.K., at the Gates of Dawn.* I heard him, as I've said, in the first movement of the Ninth: intimations, treadings, undulations, thunderous announcements, wind-in-the-willow breezes and then from way back Pan's pipes breaking through, fading away, returning, fading: an audible epiphany. I wish whoever heard it too would write to me.

* Grahame, *The Wind in the Willows*.

As Cynthia Ozick's "Pagan Rabbi" falls, calamitously, in love with a dryad, the external soul of trees, so am I, also a Jewish pagan, quite buoyantly in love with music, the external soul of human beings. Then why, contrary to my heritage, don't I have guilt feelings for my felicitous artifact-idolatry, like the poor rabbi who hangs himself for his ruinous nature-worship? The answer comes as close to explaining me to myself as anything could: Despite Jewish mothers way way back, I'm not one-hundred percent Jewish: I leave well enough alone, and trust the Powers-That-Be to do likewise.

Here's my most personal cause for modesty: My life is sustained by music. I'd like to live in a world that *is* music. But in that realm I'd not be a composer, nor performer, nor even an arranger, but just a side-lined appreciator, part of that only contingently necessary crew who sustain others' activity by their own receptivity. I learned from a bunch of nuns in a monastery whom I used to know that one could consider oneself at the all-moving center of the world just by reason of a passion, a possession by love. But they were by profession humble (by temperament, not so very), and I'm not much for humility; it is literally a lowering virtue which ends up in domination, while modesty merely bestows a certain dignity, that of self-knowledge without compensatory kudos. So I'll take that.

Why, he* asks himself, do I invest bitter labor in composing verse and song? And for once, the music itself answers, literally:

> So that it might lighten your pitiable lot
> *UT*   *RE*levet   *MI*serum *FA*tum
>
> and routine labors.
> *SO*litosque   *LA*bores.

And he hauls himself up the hexachord with bow dragging across the catgut, while ascending the diatonic scale with stately ease—a familiar doubling of the working soul's self-apprehension: weighed down by its toil, yet raised up by its art.

*Francesco Mario Veracini, Canon from *Sonate Accademiche* (1774).

28   PHILOSOPHY

Truly: You can't *study* philosophy, because then it's not philosophy, loving to think, but learnedness, becoming knowledgeable in others' thinking. You can't *do* philosophy because then it's either audacious doing-it-in or ingenious vermiculate-production. What *is* permitted to us is faithful futzing. Succinctly: a professional philosopher is a walking self-contradiction; stay a dilettante.

Amateur philosophy: deep-delving questions and messy answers. Professional philosophy: narrow-framed questions and neat answers.

Wisdom will appear as a compromise in practice, but it has originated as principle in thought.

From spontaneous thought to artful articulation: *kenosis*,* a relinquishment by materialization.

*The very high paradigm: *kenosis* (Greek: "emptying") is the term for Jesus's leaving the form of God and being incarnated.

On re-reading Kierkegaard's *Philosophical Fragments*, forty years later with much more sympathy: It is a terrific conversion-tract. In opposing a not unrecognizable Pagan Socrates to an almost brutally conceptualized Jesus ("The Paradox") he seals my conviction that this, his deliberately complex faith, here set out so superintelligently and hyperspecifically, is exactly the antithesis of what erects my soul. On the other hand, I notice a certain kinship, lesser to greater, with him: I too think "individually," meaning I'm hooked on eccentric thoughts that seem to me central—he calls them "crotchets"—stubborn, whimsical, untimely notions. Or maybe perennial, original, atemporal? Whoa, there!

Whatever others may make their vaunt: I am not the originator of my mentations. They come, or not. Are they sent or self-originating? However many may be subserved by my brain, are there yet others that are not? All that is unknown to me and to *any* other human, neuroscientist and layperson. In any case, I'm not the "creator." All I get to do is: be invitingly suggestible, concentratedly focused, discerningly selective. *In medias res* some efforts are up to me: to collect, connect, sever, replace, form, transform. And finally, it's my part to find the words—though whence *they* come, I don't know either. (However, when they go missing, I have a means of hunting them down: my old Roget's *Thesaurus*, given me by my oldest friend around 1950. It is brilliantly organized on the basic world-principle: opposition; when I can't find the right word I sneak up on it from the other side.)

So my experience of thinking implies views currently proscribed: 1. Thoughts are not aboriginally verbal, but words must be fitted to them, and, as "clothes make the man," this verbal investment, while first making the thought presentable at all, also modifies, even cloaks, its aspect. 2. There are "thoughts," thought-substances, and then there are "thinkings," thought-relations.* Both come on their own, but thinking about, with, through them is, once again, my business.

Reader—it's a confession: I'm an amateur; my Ph.D. diploma tells a lie—not for being a *Philosophiae* Doctor, "learned in *lovable wisdom*," was it bestowed on me, but for cluing out the dates of ancient potsherds—and, what was far more fun, discerning workshops and painters' hands (all highly circumstantial and wildly speculative).

* Just reminded by re-reading William James' short *Psychology* for our Senior Seminar: It's *all* in there—but nonetheless, it's mine. Well, if anything is.

Flaws in a putative being function as an existence proof, not because of the innocuous fact that to have faults you have to be, but because defects are essential to an existence in our world, or it would not be finite, hence not this-worldly.—We are affected with ontological original sin.

Having thought this laboriously out, it occurs to me that it's the complement to Anselm's proof of God's existence: He *must* exist because His *maximality* draws in every quality including existence—on the plausible hypothesis that existence *adds* something to a being, that it is, as the philosophers say, an "accident," from *ad* and *cadere*, "to accrue to." We *can* exist only because our *finitude*, evident in our deficiencies and defects, is the very condition of our being here and now, that is, of mortal existence.

Coming-to-be and passing-away: Are these eventuations or continua, moments or evolvings? In the soul's time, the former, in the clock's time, the latter, so both at once: We live, really live, leaping from event to event, but exist, *are really here and now,** creeping in unmarked stretches between.

*I'm again reading *Being and Time* but won't apologize to its author for retrieving "existence" for its traditional meaning; coming last doesn't accord culmination-rights.

Sertillanges says of the mind that "passivity is its first law."* It's a bold locution for affective readiness, alert receptivity. But: whence comes the fulfilling consignment—and can you ever count on its arriving? That's not to be settled in this life, but we may, indeed must, have our conjectures. One purpose of dying is corroboration.

* *The Intellectual Life.*

A contradiction in terms: Willful philosophy. Neither my will, nor thy will, nor anyone's will should have a thing to do with it.

There are people, writers too, who think that truth equals exposure and that verity is certified by denigration. They can, oddly, be stylistically magnificent—Lucretius, Hobbes, Nietzsche. Lucretius does worse than deny the gods, he depreciates them by distance and disassociation; they're inoperative wraiths. Yet he has a presiding deity, voluptuous Venus; but then again the whoring women under her regime are repulsive. He clears the world of everything but atomic matter, then he builds an absurdity into the initial state of his physics, the parallel *downpour* of atoms through an infinite, *directionless* vacuum. The originally non-impinging particles are brought into cohesive conformations by a causeless proto-swerve. Thereafter he offers, insouciantly, multiple explanations for the phenomena of this supposedly reductionist world, and resorts to brute sensationalism such as a sun the size of two-finger-breadths. He likes sitting on a coastal hill watching ships capsize in a storm; his poem's climax is a horrible plague,* and for all that, his materialism is to bring peace of mind. Maybe by reading some really terrific Latin poetry?

Hobbes means to work a similar magic by mordant truths exhilaratingly told in terms arrestingly defined. Here's my favorite: Laughter is *"Sudden glory"*—caused by "the apprehension of a deformed thing in another that makes us applaud ourselves in comparison."† Q.E.D.

Nietzsche, dangerously off in his prescriptive prognostications, is hilariously on-point in his verbal skewerings of our modernity.

* Symptoms courtesy of Thucydides.
† *Leviathan.*

I don't understand Nietzsche: Why choose for your prime term of approbation not *edel,* "noble," but *vornehm,** "elegant, fashionable"—a term with which to praise young ladies.

* *Beyond Good and Evil.* Well, actually I can guess why: German *vornehm* = Latin *praecipuus,* so literally: "taken before," and originally: "exclusive, surpassing, foremost."

Plato is a writer whose dialogues were subtitled by some clueless eager beaver in antiquity, some as "peirastic" (tentative), some as "aporetic" (perplexed). I think there are no hesitant or stymied Socratic inquiries; every dialogue has an answer to its question or to the question that ought to have been asked. Sometimes it's in the *action* of the participants, in what their talk is doing—to them, to their listeners, to us. Sometimes it's hidden in a *throwaway* for normally acute readers to catch on to. Sometimes it's in plain sight as a *paradox* that rightly read turns into higher-level wisdom. A *very* bad idea: to write a book systemically setting out the positive truth in each of the thirty-six, bad precisely because it *could* be done; it would be outing Socrates' pedagogic tact. But it's irresistible.

Esoteric writing in philosophy: love's labor lost. Why go for exclusionary deviousness and multileveled discourse when the matter itself is forbiddingly difficult? Besides, how do you know the ones who get it are your most desirable disciples? Or that the world doesn't suspect funny business anyhow?*

* *Exempli gratia*: Leibniz, regarded by esotericists as a *crypto*-atheist, was (I read somewhere) known by the locals as *Löwenitz*, "Believe-nothing."

The examined life: *Behold* what you see and *regard* what you notice. Apropos of a keen-eyed, noticingly unregarding friend in her New England mode: "Yes, I wondered about that," meaning: "None of my business." I think Socrates means: "Everything around me is my business, and it keeps me too locally busy for touristic travel."

Is there such an item as a pure thought in either sense—purely a thought (without an admixture of sense or affect) or a pure thought (without taint of some self-serving)? I've read of it, but to me it would seem a soul-constricting event.

Moderns I know tend to treat myths as reusable heirlooms, relieved of the conviction, belief, and mystery once attached to them, now fixed up as scene-settings for current preoccupations. All right, but here's the price: grand visions have turned into didactic narratives, vivid pictures into prosing parables, and what philosophy has gained in *sophia*, cleverness,* it has lost in *philia*, amiability.

* *Sophia* properly means "cleverness, craft, skill"; "wisdom" is a derivative sense.

I'm at bottom persuaded that there is a transcendental order that informs the here and now, but my faith and its reasons regularly abscond. Well, my intellect isn't a book in which I must read the same text on Monday through Friday as on Saturday or Sunday, whichever is my day of coming-to. As long as I do come to.

Sometimes the integrated cosmos breaks up into an incongruous chaos. Is it me disintegrating or the world unmasking itself? Is it scarier to recognize that I, who am essentially incompetent to be, *have* to be, or that the world doesn't know what or why it is? I think the latter, since I'm the more promising venue for amendment.

I suspect that Aristotle is more intellectually acute than Plato and Plato than Socrates. So then why is my order of adherence the reverse? Because plausible access to transcendence depends more on imaginative largeness than on intellectual ingenuity. Thus Aristotle is, precisely by his careful avoidance of flights of fancy, for example, by the very logic of his analysis of natural motion,* ultimately driven into the wild blue yonder of his all-moving, hands-off *Nous*, fraught with more mind-boggling wonders than are the Socratic forms with dialectical problems.

* *Physics.*

Paradox is not ambiguity, being a staunchly clear self-contradiction, not a waffling indefiniteness. So also does transient uncertainty differ from settled indeterminacy, the former being a virtue of the inquiring intellect, the second a—no, *the*—vice of thinking, which *ought to* seek *terminal finality.* As hypocrisy is the respect virtue pays to vice,* so uncertainty is the respect a soul pays to its finitude. Moreover, as even defective virtue enacted is preferable to its mere acknowledgment, so sometimes even precipitous conclusions are sounder than premeditated waffling.

Why, on the other hand, even my ultimate convictions should have a penumbra of personal uncertainty: 1. simple—I could be wrong, from sheer personal limitation; 2. complex—I could be right, but only limitedly so, from the inherent logical delimitations of any determinate position. (This thought acknowledges the *non*-Systematic Hegelianism of life.)

* La Rochefoucauld.

Why does every "putting of the question" expect two sides? Why not?

Unending question: Is the truth ultimately or only intermediately paradoxical? A possible way of burking the question: if contradictory dualities were to be finally self-resolving, meaning that ultimate antitheses are compassed not from beyond but from within. But Heraclitus, our first searcher, was willing to proclaim an even more mind-boggling case: self-opposition as *the vital way of ultimate being*.

Sudden awakening from a hot and heavy afternoon nap, as if driven out of sleep by my own heartbeat: a moment of absolutely threadbare reality before regained consciousness respins its own cocooning hominess. Am I meant to extract an ontology from it? (I've been preparing for my Heidegger preceptorial, hence this mood-hermeneutics.) If so, would it be: There *is a bare, a mere world* awaiting our investment—our first business on awaking?

The limitations on openness are stiff pride, specific desire, entrenched againstness. But these are also aspects of self-preservation, said to be the first law of nature by one of our founding philosophers.* So perhaps the requirements of our intellectual and political nature are out of kilter?—No "perhaps," but perhaps reconcilable.

* Hobbes, *Leviathan*.

Why sometimes the unique instance most truly represents its kind: because in its near-inarticulable "specificity" it is an *arresting* example of its species.

Are the depths brighter or murkier than the shallows? Aristotle's answer adapted: Things clearer in themselves are darker to us.* Our labor is to delineate them as clearly as possible in their very inaccessibility, in the faith that Down- or Up-there is free of accreted complexity.

* *Physics* I.1: "The way is naturally from what is more known to us and clearer to what is clearer by nature and more knowable."

Nietzsche's *Ecce Homo*: Incipient madness seems to be the pivot point on which selective reticence turns into uncensored self-revelation—wherewith a genius can captivate and confuse a continent. Nietzsche's case shows that having genius and being great (I mean beneficent) are not the same.

A man fighting gallantly to lever a delicate stomach into a spiritual asset attracts, besides my admiration, my pity, surely so unwelcome to its object as to be more an act of aggression than of understanding. The truth is that all the talk of halcyon days, golden moments, serene distance, seems willed to me, and that the all fulminations of heaven-scaling outrageousness, the blue smoke of abysmal subtlety, seem like desperate self-exaltations.

Once more, *re* Nietzsche. God save us from the philosophic geniuses with poor enteric constitutions: rude-health worship levered into truth-devotion. But careful: even a little good sense will tell you not to construe digestive luck as truth-relevant superiority.

Two types, guess my preference: 1. Regards perennially recurrent puzzles, in-principle unanswerable questions, probably insoluble problems, as time-wasters; gets on with research you can frame in effective terms. 2. Considers what is beyond us as our special (species-appropriate) business, a. because you don't know if it's so fruitless till you try (since it's not public progress but personal substance that's at stake), and b. because that's what the time (or more sensibly, some time) of our lives is for—what else, really?

I have little faith either in the philosophers who want to *do in* philosophy or in those who claim to *do* it (Wittgenstein, Ryle). It's not an assault or a labor, for heaven's sake. (Well, one might object, it was Kant, the real thing, who declares somewhere, proudly, that philosophy has now learned to be work—though, then again, he says otherwise elsewhere.)

The courage of the First philosophers (First in time and, not coincidentally, First in ontology*): to proclaim, really on no better grounds than that Being has evidential looks ("knowledge-shapes"†) to testify to its being, while Nothing has only treacherous speech ("Nothing *is*") to assert its existence, the primacy of the former. That's the ontological bias of the West, and henceforth *pro* always takes precedence over *con*, and the nothingists (nihilists) are forever, *ipso facto*, second to the ontologists—consigned to intrinsic reaction.

* Which deals with what is primary in Being.

† *Eide*, "forms" or "aspects," from a Greek verb that has two roots for different tenses, one meaning "see," the other, "know." I have heard it argued that this linguistic fact determined Plato's philosophy and its progeny. But what determined the linguistic fact? And why "determined" rather than "inspired"?

I have an insuperable addiction to what my linguistic ancestors call the *Drum und Dran*, circumstantial expansiveness—in fiction and my own musings, that is. In philosophy, it's: Get to it.

The headlong briskness of daily doing versus the halting essays of persistent thought: Life flies and leaves you sleepy; thought traipses and leaves you tired.

People know that it's—somewhat—easier for us to intellectualize passion than to impassion the intellect. The former mode is called "rationalizing" and is considered a peculiar Western propensity. But that doesn't quite work. Even "ideology," the crudest of rationalisms, is, after all, the chokehold desire has on thought.

I saw a journalist on TV, speculating away in this vein while standing—obscuringly—in front of some Western boys who'd thrown themselves into the embrace of the Islamic State. One of them—unregarded in the half-hidden background—gave it all away: "It cures depression." He wasn't escaping *from* creeping rationalism but *to* numbing frenzy.

Fly in the bottle*—bee in the bonnet. If people have got the latter, that's what they should let out. To Wittgenstein: that buzzing fly he wants to discharge—it's his soul.

* *Philosophical Investigations* 309.

Our *Umwelt*, the world surrounding us, is a "buzzing confusion,"* indefinite in extent, filled with oppositions, antitheses, contraries, contradictions—all different ways of being at odds with itself—not to speak of indeterminacies, indecidabilities, both inherent and epistemological (in themselves and for us). Each one of us marks the center of all this welter, and each is responsible for making some local sense for ourselves and entitled to infer a wider order for our world, a world informed by its initial localism: That's the niche principle, which says that depending on our powers of inference and conjecture a niche can acquire global scope. Thus, I might say, the world becomes my oyster (if oyster-insides weren't so squishily, repulsively unkosher).

* William James.

Leave Being whole: when you affirm something, include the consequences.

Some thoughts I borrow, some I concoct, the ones I care about just come—do I have *any* part in their birth? Well, yes, sometimes they stick out a limb and I get the hands of my mind (Augustinian locution!) around them and pull—that's all. Now here's the enigma: It's exactly the same experience that makes me think they're really *mine*.

Now let Socrates speak of *his* midwifery: The babies he delivered are his youngsters' brain-children.* More: he can tell if they are true-born children or spectres to be exposed by him. For his own part, he is totally "ungenerative of wisdom" (*agonos sophias*)—the dedicated teacher's crafty abnegation: The boys bear; he only culls.

* *Theaetetus* 150.

Are there people who can't think deeply, ever? No, it's rarely intellectual disability, but the temperamental incapacity for prolonged focusing, for that sustained dis-ease by which our interest outstays the first diffusive engagement, when the strings of concentration aren't yet taut and tuned. After that, it's more feasible to fiddle and futz and worm our way into the matter than not to—those being the modes of ingress known to me.

I've seen two sorts of wisdom: *implicit*—intuitive, immediate, wordless, and *explicit*—thoughtful, protracted, articulate. They're usually found in distinct individuals. Now when they come together in one—that is an all-purpose human being.

Why is clarity of thought quite compatible with satisfyingly brisk flexibility, while muddle-headedness tends to an annoyingly elusive rigidity? Because when people see where they're going they stride freely and avoid obstacles easily, but if they're in a fog they get uptight and step inhibitedly.

Once again, the diversions of professional philosophy: to turn exploratory futzing-around with a deep, origin-seeking question into a precise, hard-edged treatment of a well-delimited problem.

There's an art to stating a quandary; it involves framing perplexities determinately enough to direct an inquiry but not so terminally as to forestall it.

Augustine, whom I cherish, says: "*Nulla est homini causa philosophandi, nisi ut beatus sit,*" a perfectly phrased intimation of what I call ontological optimism: "A human being has no cause for philosophizing except that he may be blessed."* Yet I'd revise it radically: "A human being has no *right* to philosophize *unless* he *is* happy." The undoubtedly deep reflections of distressed authors have done a lot of harm—best but not only example: Rousseau, he of totalitarian wish-fulfillment. Of course these martyrs of the intellect should produce books, say of melancholiac meditations, just not of political philosophy, or worse, of ontology; it's too often me-ontology—the English looks serendipitous, but that's merely fortuitous: *me* is Greek for "non-".

* *City of God.*

I think philosophy is more alert naiveté than strained sophistication.

Life should be stripped down and thinking full of curlicues, so that thinking will be adequate and life rich.

My thinking is really small beer; that's not modesty but realism. But there's this to say for it: It's home-grown, and down-home is better than up-high. But, really: home-grown? Can a reading person's thinking be her own? And then again: Can a bookless person's thinking go far? Damned if you do, damned if you don't. The half-happy solution is that if it's too late to undo it on purpose, it's never too soon for spontaneous forgetfulness.

29 PLAINTS

The wisdom that suffering makes you better is mostly a compensatory sockdolager of souls in pain. What makes you good is happiness rightly understood. Aeschylus, mighty testifier, says, to be sure: *pathos mathos*, "suffering is learning."* Well, for choral bystanders or for the occasional hero.

Agamemnon. Probably more correctly read inversely; students may grin knowingly, but *that* isn't what he means.

What is the use of squawking about the world, or trumpeting the joys of another, when you can't tell people what's best to do this afternoon?—which is usually to fix something or study something or phone somebody. What's next? is the most urgent question and requires an immediately practical answer—always for children (as we kindergarten teachers know, oh so well) and often for distressed grown-ups. And yet in the long run of life, it's just the opposite: The question "What to do with myself?" should be formed and answered way ahead of now's exigencies, and "What to do after lunch?" should be determined—go lightly here—*sub specie aeternitatis*.

Exemplar of the mixed motive: not complaining 1. from consideration, so as not to burden friends, 2. from cravenness, so as to forestall inattention.

Small satisfactions are wonderful fillers for the holes left by large disappointments. (Not for everyone; only those willing to turn in tragedy-kudos for commonplace comfort.)

Grand calamity, called tragedy, may well be a make-or-break learning episode, but quotidian life is the best schooling for what, after all, the victim of tragic grandeur presumably hopes for—eventless ordinariness.

You feel miserable. Dump on someone. Now they feel worse (if they're nice) and you better. If they feel only *derivatively* bad and you feel better *in propria persona*, it's a fair bargain.

Part of the relief in telling one's troubles is that the teller is—the more restrained, the more effectively—swathing herself in pathos, a perfectly permissible arrogation of dignity, and very therapeutic.

German: *Pechvogel*, "pitch-bird," one prone to bad luck. But is it luck to keep getting into the tar? Or is it an anti-gift, so to speak, a tar-talent? In any case, it's double trouble—their perpetual problems and my ever-sticky sympathy. It's troublingly sad when a person's very being gives you the willies.

Shouldn't complain—because when you're miserable and do complain to another, if he's made miserable by your misery, then you've got twice as many miserable people, and if he isn't made miserable by your misery, then you're now twice as miserable yourself.

A comfort: distress is not always in proportion to objective misfortune—less at its upper end; I've had two friends who flinched at and fussed over life's little miseries for scores of years and then met an evil diagnosis with perfect sang-froid.

It's invoking trouble, personal and political, to call for dispensations on the plea of previous suffering. You're arousing pity, forgetting how close it is to irritation, and worse, contempt. Moreover, a victim has, by definition, been injured and is classified as handicapped.

People who glow in the glare of tragedy often dim under the twilight of the resolution.

Complainy-ness, continual briefing of your friends on your griefs and grievances, wears out sympathy—that fellow-feeling based on human solidarity and bucked up, truth to tell, by curiosity.

Grudge-carrying is the sclerosis of the faculty of indignation.

Here's a really healthy obsession: capturing experiences—be it of thing, event, image, or motion of the soul—with the most complete exactitude of detail and precision of delineation. This is one non-stymieing perfectionism. It produces relief, since suffering accurately articulated is suffering safely contained, since joy minutely described is joy soundly preserved, since opposition truthfully expounded is opposition securely boxed in—and so on.

The program of leveraging deficiencies into distinctions gives me the willies. I'm all for people finding relief where they can, but I won't be bamboozled into bad-is-good think. "Because of" is plain Pollyannaism; "despite of" has a touch of heroism. But then again, for the protagonist of a private tragedy, it may be a distinction without a difference.

Is there private tragedy in the grand sense? Doesn't it require a *mise en scène*? Private tragedy is better termed misery; it lacks the production values. That's really true of the tragic figures themselves—being Antigone in public, defiantly heroic, is surely more magnificent than being Antigone by herself, privately having to deal with it.

Hard fact: usually suffering diminishes, even demeans us. But when it irradiates the soul, a wonder ensues and a cause for love.

30   PRIVACY

Whoever values privacy, the *hortus conclusus** of the soul, had better abstain from that deliberate opacity called secretiveness. It attracts curiosity and conjecture.

*The medieval walled garden, a place of delight, enclosed to exclude uninitiated humans and wild beasts (except the unicorn).

These look alike and are worlds apart: inhibitedness—the *inability* to let the soul appear, and reserve—the *unwillingness*. They're as subservience is to sovereignty, unease to serenity. And the one is apt to end in the messy ruin of wild explosion, the other in the sweet flow of controlled release.

Of course (well, it used to be) we want privacy, to hide our misdeeds, indulgences, indelicacies. That's basic, but not central. Central is the need to be un-inspected, simply unwatched, to be "by" ourselves. It's the necessary predicate for coming out into sociability.

Does a stereotype (originally a printing plate) abstract from reality or print it out? Female formulas, for instance, are sometimes roughly realized in reality: steely belle (bravo!) or sugar-and-spice-and-everything-nice girlie-girl (yecch!). But isn't that *self-presentation*, as when at a fun fair, for an old-style photo, you stick your face through one of those full-sized generic cartoons with a hole, while behind it you're unclassifiably individual? But then again: your front may belie your interior, but it says *something*. Hurrah for stereotypes and the folks that fit them; if humanity were individualistic without remainder, there'd be no novels.

In youth our confiding is a big deal (as older confidants ought to recall)—because we view ourselves as both hopelessly and hopefully unique (bad locution, good point); we're self-important and vulnerable. That's mostly gone late in life: We're canonical beings, and confidences are anecdotes. What a relief for ourselves and our auditors (in the listening and in the inspecting sense)!

Human orneriness: We zealously guard a secret for half a century, then casually let it out one fine day. Because it was no longer active? Or, reversely, because its valve finally blew? Or even because what was once a source of shame is now a fount of prestige?

"Undemonstrative" is often the opposite of "inexpressive."

What would be the point of talking silently to yourself at length if not to make utterance to others have point and concision? No, that's false. First it's to find out how your floating apprehensions do when they're word-tethered.

What a calamity when the day arrives (as it well may) when an implanted electronic app will give utterance to one's internal speech—perhaps (who knows what people will submit to) willy-nilly, as now in cyberfiction. The incessant rounds of personal hurt feelings (when responses escape before revision) and political persecutability (because of terminal transparency)—those will be the gross horrors; the more delicate and more devastating loss will be that of self-communing, of producing for one's own, sole entertainment, wit and wisdom not so remarkable when externalized, of indulging in self-pleasing, imaginative repetition (otherwise called day-dreaming), of having an ultimate hiding place—what the British so elegantly call a funk-hole. In other words: no truly inner life.

Maxim: Reserve gives tautness to human relations. The therapeutically inclined infantilization of people includes the breakdown of their reluctance to tell all, with possible temporary relief now—but certain desolation later. (Discovery at Columbine:* inducing children to rehearse horrors may reinforce the trauma.)

*School shooting in Colorado, 1999.

Candor in communication seems, sensibly, to vary directly with the copiousness of psychic life. Meager souls must keep something in stock.

Only marginally on-point.—Me: "I'll give you a piece of my mind." My brother: "Can you spare it?"

If you want your privacy, be utterly candid and completely discreet. Meaning: Don't incite probings with teasing intimations, and do turn off questions by clear refusals. Danger: As in youth inhibition holds too much too close, in old age sang-froid might let too much out.

Moll Flanders* (a woman who knows all the world but not herself) says: "a Secret Moment should always have a Confident, a bosom friend . . ." She's right, but it had best be oneself, who is certainly a bosom friend and no blabberer to boot.

* Defoe.

Private : public :: self-appearance : self-representation : being : acting :: coming-to : going-out :: withdrawing : extending :: laying-up : laying out :: gathering : expending.

With intimates, we can be ourselves, meaning we relax— well, no; we are energetically at ease. In privacy, we go taut—or rather we're on the *qui vive*. For what? For our disrobed silly, panicky, resentful, vengeful, wise, inerrantly masterful, unrealistically generous, grandly forgiving selves.

We say a lot to ourselves we wouldn't expect or accept from our friends. Why? Surely not because their judgment would be harder on us than our own or less profitable, but, I think, because what is announced out loud in a real room resonates through time, in two memories, whereas what is said in the muted volume of inner quasi-space is soon overlaid by our non-stop self-talk—and relegated to the one memory that we administer.

Reserved comfort is like a cool, dry hand.

The "inner sanctum" is actually quite unholy and not so secluded; here, held in their protective custody, its secrets are dying to come out. You have but to ask at the right moment in the right way. And its infections, here segregated in their isolation ward, are longing for sociability; misery loves company.—The *effective* desire for privacy marks a not so common humanity.

Nothing attracts confidences like the prospect of un-avid listening. And for that, the older the better: You've had your fill of fascinating revelations but they have not yet drawn down all your sympathy.

Once again: public vs. private. Surely the usual antitheses apply: large vs. small, common vs. particular, social vs. individual. But perhaps above all: what we do vs. what we feel. It's surely the case that the forum is the venue of action; there even speech is deed. But as it's a good place for staged emoting, so it's bad for more subtle affect—a venue where every motion of the soul is stultified: stilted or crudified (a word of attested usage because I've just used it).

TWO OVERLAPPING MEDITATIONS ON PRIVACY

WHY PRIVACY?

The question becomes urgent because the loss of privacy in the cyberworld is insouciantly foretold and sanguinely accepted.

1. Is what is forgone here actually privacy? The indiscreet self-disclosures and the indecent outings might haunt or harry self-perpetrators or others' victims.

But these are harms to reputation, not to true privacy. So acceptance of one's own indiscretions coming to light, indifference to world-wide exposure, is probably the default strategy. What I mean to say is that the exposures of cyberspace and the forced, consequent shamelessness pertain to an only secondary sort of privacy, which might be called *public privacy*, such as has to do with disclosure of personal information and divulging of intended secrets, matters that personal discretion or public law might affect.

But there is also a *primary privacy* which might be indirectly tainted by the collapse of "public" privacy, the truly private privacy (from Latin *privus*, "single").

2. Will human nature, which has for millennia had a dual aspect, that of an exposable and of an intimate self, one day soon find itself devoid of this primary private part, this singularity, which already is a generation along the way?

Thoughtless application of the term "evolution" makes these changes appear to be adaptive, natural. But true evolutionary change is secularly, naturally slow; the fast, forced, Lamarckian* outcomes of accommodation to recent circumstances might be maladaptive. For practical current purposes human nature may be fixed, so that new mental modes might be *deformations* rather than *adaptations*. Will the collapse of human duality and the resorption of the intimate, private self into a psychic appendix be such a degeneration?

3. So then, is privacy, privative, unexposed living, of the human essence? Would its adaptive evanescence

be a human calamity? Well, recall a night of "opening up," "telling all," even to a trusted fellow human. Wasn't there a thinning of substance, an evacuation of the soul? Density of inner being comes in part from hoarding one's being and holding one's self close.

4. Moreover, there's the sense of falsification, of omitting and skewing, that dogs even the most sincere desire to come clean. "The truth, the whole truth, and nothing but the truth" is neither in us nor for us: we don't really know it and we couldn't finitely say it. In sum: our inner store is depletable *and* traducable. Hence the need for regenerative and concealing privacy.

5. Or rather, semi-privacy. Intimate communication not only disburdens the heart and lightens it; it also erects the soul, as it basks in admiration and pity—the sort that makes a warrior say: "She loved me for the dangers I had pass'd / And I loved her that she did pity them."† But such communing privacy depends on privative privacy, on sessions of sweet silent thought.

6. Confidences are, as the word says, acts of faith, and so they are often confessions of our misdeeds and (this is harder) of our anomalies. Telling one's sins, probably more often of omission than commission, is self-absolution; one's confidant (or confidante) needs, unlike a confessing priest, only to hear, as if a sin aired were a sin dissipated—no *ego absolvo te*, that's not a friend's office. As for the hidden deviances of individual personality (as distinct from the commonalities of personhood), a friend of the heart will declare them lovable. (The harsh truth is that the victim

of visible abnormalities can demand normalization from now till doomsday. Before God, it might happen, not here in public. But perhaps in intimate privacy. On earth, the bearer is marked, stigmatized, and bears the tag "special," the ultimate euphemism, since here "special" can't possibly mean "favored" and since the species is precisely not so branded. There is a politically correct rebranding not universally appreciated; I served on a State Civil Rights Commission with a severely crippled man—I represented Woman (Jews weren't in it), he the Challenged—who said to me: "My distinction is that I live as a cripple, and now they want to take that away from me." Am I straying?

7. Well, the point is that we all are and feel deviant (I imagine) and wish to consign that fact—even if we rejoice in it—to the deepest privacy: "An ill-favored thing, sir, but mine own."‡ Privacy screens the double life we endow with glee and trepidation. (The Latin source, *privus*, means both "single" and "peculiar.")

8. There is a *noli me tangere* mode to our inwardness, a touch-me-notism. Why? Inwardness is both tough and delicate: like fine glass, it resonates without shattering, but it is vulnerable to the imprint of fingerings. It is prone to shame—preventively ashamed of being put to shame by intrusive impertinences. This is the classless aristocracy of the soul; it shows up most poignantly in the best of the young.

9. Similarly there's a certain esthetic exclusivity, a not altogether reasonable recalcitrance to visitations. The well-cultivated soul is a *hortus conclusus*, that secret garden that's closed to trampling visitors, most of all to would-be walk-ins.

10. Keeping secrets, once more, being secretive, has little to do with psychic privacy. If you've been indiscreet, the best strategy is to anticipate disclosure and go public. (A good example: Wowi [Wovereit], styled the "reigning burgomaster" of my hometown Berlin, came out as gay before his subsequent long tenure, and interest in exposing his private life blessedly collapsed.) In fact, the best preventive of intrusive interest is to tell copiously—it forestalls being heard. If you've been sufficiently discreet, don't let on that there's a secret; nothing attracts intrusive attention more than a secret known only *as* a secret. In any case, sound souls don't have secrets but privacies. From the aspect of primary privacy the difference between secrets and privacies is that the former you don't want *others to know*, while the latter you don't want *yourself to tell*.

11. Aristotle says the most wonderful thing:§ friendship depends on a—highly specified—self-love. A self-friend finds himself *again* in another. (I am, although it's Aristotle as says so, a little dubious of the alter-ego theory of friendship; I don't need two of me). Yet this future friend of another finds himself *first* in pleasing solitude, and this seems wonderfully observed. So privacy is the prep-school of friendship, and there also are stored our reserves, our designated contributions to friendship, our best disposable riches.

* Lamarckian evolution: Acquired traits are heritable.
† *Othello.*
‡ *As You Like It.*
§ *Nicomachean Ethics.*

PRIVACY: NOTES OF A CONVERSATION
WITH TWO OLD FRIENDS

(Santa Fe, July 2014)

Is reticence, the withholding of internalities, the reserving of one's own to oneself, guarded privacy—is this condition necessary to a sound human life? Is it degraded and diminished by full disclosure, boundless publicity? Don't soul-professionals preach that "talking it out" makes things better? (Some, to be sure, have discovered that it can make things worse, for instance, as mentioned, for children present at school shootings; let sleeping dogs lie). Is casually careless surrender of privacy an urgent danger to our common humanity or just a life-style indulgence for those who don't care and so aren't harmed?

Anyhow, for now the public framing of the danger is mostly haphazardly circumstantial. The culpably innocent young post indiscretions that will cause immediate embarrassment, invite predators, and dog them into adulthood, being essentially unerasable, privacy law notwithstanding. As a tranquilizer, the priests of universal informational access preach the welcome demise of shame; consequently the young cyberpublic, adrift between a now proscribed embarrassment and an ineradicable sense of vulnerability, goes terminally anxious. So people worry— "on a case by case basis," as they say. Serious public concern is with privacy in terms of security: identity theft and invasions of accounts.

The effect on human ways of being is very lightly touched on—who's got the time?

What really is properly public? Well, identity, by its very name: "Self-sameness" is subject to "identification," which means literally "making self-same." If truth is traditionally said to be "the making adequate of thought to thing," then analogously, being yourself is now the matching of yourself to a document—you've been identified. It's an inherently public process, alright. Where you yourself and your documents are only virtually present, the match-up can be stolen, of course: identity theft. Vital information, such as name, residence, birth date, cyber-security may partially protect, *your soul's intimacies not at all*. That's up to the platoons of your online friends into whose virtual keeping you gave them.

So why hang on to a secret life? No, once again, "secret" is wrong. Secrets are self-consciously maintained, in fear or pride; those who let on that they have a secret must secretly hope to be compromised. The life we mean should rather be called *intimate*, "deep within." If an inviolably intimate life is of the human essence—now considered not as an ontological but as a psychological question, more in line with my two friends' propensities—then what should we keep in mind?

Well, we each and severally declare (though the phrasing is mine):

1. I should not by the soul's evacuation invite psychic implosion.

2. I should not collude in my own misinterpretation— which a "true confession" would unavoidably be.

3. The world's view of me should be balanced by my self-interpretation, devised in inviolable seclusion.

4. The diversions of the world should be supplemented by the re-creations of solitude.

What makes the coursing car such an apt confessional—eyes front; speech sideways—is that it provides a fine, safe sort of togetherness: side-*by*-side, seating parallel, taking in the passing scene / side-*to*-side, address orthogonal, responding to a transient confidence—the perfect constellation for tactful communion—bowling swiftly through the world, attending discreetly to a friend.

"Our eye-beames twisted, and did thred / Our eyes upon one double string."* Here, resting upon the swelling bank of violets, two people are differently configured, for utter, wordless eye-to-eye intimacy. Can't do that in a car, got to mind the road.—Probably the more interesting togetherness, in the long run.

* Donne, "The Ecstasie," quoted above.

Reticence raises curiosity; candor kills it. For those who really want their privacy: casually tell all.

Between talking to a deaf or a too avid ear, I'll take the former—but wish for the middle, the discreetly hearing ear.

Yes, telling evacuates experiences, but it also actualizes them. In coming out into the light of common life they lose their penumbral murk and are cut down to size—but in compensation they're now a fact of social life.

Telling airs out experience, dissipates its aroma, sweet or rank, like a sweaty shirt that's been through the washing machine—no longer reminiscently pungent and much less mine (well, when I used to jog).

Any aloneness is better than bad togetherness, but not for everybody, I guess. Rather the occasional melancholy of anechoic space than the continual irritation of unwanted proximity.

Once again, sound reticence: not secretive but private, not fearing disclosures but cherishing treasures.

In some people "reserve" stems from a fear of expending limited internal resources. But communicative ebullience doesn't always betoken confidence in indefinite psychic replenishment. Sometimes it's just bubbles of expressiveness, rising up from that simmering pot in the midriff.

Screened passion issues as human warmth, suppressed feeling as stiff distance.

I think of myself as *both* obsessively introspective, fixated on keeping my psychic house in order, *and*, again, freely flying over the roof of my life without having tracked down what's what, why, how, and the number of ways I fool myself. This dual mode of tense trying and relieved relinquishing has a saving grace—makes me feel friendly toward my fellow-messers-about.

When you tell your life to avid anecdote-collectors, if you want to be credible there should be a moment, an insert, as it were, of darkness, an unhappiness, a plumb bob exhibiting gravity. Yet if you do oblige, it'll be over-heard—which was, I guess, your intention. Those who notice are welcome to more: by now everything happened back in the Dark Ages (a.k.a. youth*); it's all mottled parchment and faded ink.

*Surviving which—that eventuates at about forty-five years of age—is *major bliss*. Youth has three analogous crises: the Terrible Twos (will-aggression), the Arduous Adolescence (self-agony), the Midlife Crisis (world-anxiety).

Apropos of the central one: How did I contrive to conduct a classical European-style adolescence at Bay Ridge High School for Girls in Brooklyn?

P.S. Laura, who magicks my penciled pages into electronic texts (a disappearing act), asks: What's a European-style adolescence? Here's an inventory: Chastely ardent "particular" friendship *and* snootily exclusive group-belonging; obsessive, uneasy rummaging for final truths *and* absolute certainty of the elders' obtuseness; musical rapture extracted from a narrow source (mostly Beethoven and of him, the Seventh, and of that, the second movement, "Frère Jacques" turned into a somber processional) *and* world-embracing fugue-states, intimation from bygone times that never were. In short, attained sublimation and privatized Romanticism.

Reserve: not expending your being in utterance.

31 PUSHBACK

What a blessing our human finitude is—but only when rightly understood and willingly accepted: as a warrant for formulating some problems as ultimate mysteries, without thereby putting them, as the Romans say, *ad acta*, "into the inactive file."

"You're being simplistic, naïve, defensive."—Well, you bet: I'm trying to find some push-back to your masked bullying, argumentative, complication-creating one-upmanship. I'm simplistic because you're invested in complexities, naïve because you offer banal sophistication, and defensive because you're aggressive. Some day I'll compile a Dictionary of Asymmetric Polemics. "Asymmetric," recall, is the current military adjective for terrorist warfare* that employs tactics to which one can't easily respond in kind.

* *Counterinsurgency Field Manual* 3–24.

The knock-down, drag-out put-down: "It's not so simple." Answer: "So begin to tell, I've got hours." That complexity ploy is often a mask for people's own confusion, with which it is a pleasure to infect the other: "You thought you alone had clarity; now we're both in perplexity." I think when you're in the complexity phase you should suppress speech until you're in the mode of regained simplicity. All this is for us adults. For students, you really should hear the tale, because clarification comes with telling. And often you even get the last word: "So you see, it was so simple." Emerging rule: complexity is for books; simplicity for speech.

Homo double *sapiens* seems to be dysfunctional, unadaptive as hell to his self-made environment: We like refined sugar, lots of salt, all kinds of pre-maltreated food. We like games that ruin our brains, and who loves broccoli except with loads of butter? We watch violence being done to others on screens while ourselves sitting, superlatively supine, in perfect but unhealthy safety. (Against my self-promise I say "we"—that holier-than-thou first person plural, by which I here mean *not* to signify: all of you, not me). There's one aspect to rejoice in: *Homo sapiens sapiens et sciens* is said by scientists to be beyond that humbling Descent of Man directed by natural unexceptionalist evolution.*

* E.O. Wilson predicts a period of humanly directed "voluntary evolution." Actually, I'll take nature, if it's still there for the taking. Oh, incidentally: *homo sapiens sapiens* is a species name for modern man: really wise.

Don't subvert your humanity by "*being* a something," as in "I'm a social scientist"—the subversion is accomplished in the elided "I *am*," to which we could more easily say: "Surely not."

Whatever is said in entirely good faith, no matter how wrong-headed it is, must be credited with this saving grace: that a good human soul could embrace it—for a while.

The squeaky wheel gets the grease, they say. Because it squeaks so boldly or because it creaks so rustily? It makes a big difference, you know—as a guide to one's behavior.

Idealet: meaning-deprived and word-wealthy. A subset is the concept-construct: sense-deforming and brilliance-asserting.

Intention takes, *pace* general opinion, the thwack and sting out of the slings and arrows of outrageous insult. It's easier to bear up under pointed malice than under by-the-way insult. That's because the desire to mortify secreted in a derogatory opinion nullifies its validity, while the innocent spontaneity of careless contempt testifies to its veracity.

In childhood you mayn't step on the cracks in the concrete; in adulthood you tread wherever you come down: the desacralization of the world.

I know people who never learned a thing and remember it all.

Doubt is not the sea of unknowing but a determinate difficulty about a definite point. Consequently, doubts can be resolved, but un-knowing is chronic. It used to be thought that the then mostly fatal disease of tuberculosis induced an elevated state of awareness (the premise of Mann's *Magic Mountain*), and so still does *real* agnosticism, Greek for "the state of un-knowing"; it is a chronic dis-ease you can live with. On the other hand, atheism ought to be intolerable. For to know with certainty that a thinkable Being is *not* is ontologically impossible, since the territory of Non-being is infinite by its logical nature and thus not searchable. So a believing a-theist, an "alpha-privative* goddist," to translate literally, is in the logical quicksands.

* "Alpha-privative" is the grammatician's name for the negating Greek *a*, as in "amoral," morally unfixed, to be distinguished from "immoral," plain wicked.

If you invest yourself in negation, like Milton's Satan, there's nothing left (by your own figuring) to contain you. Then you're infinite, a terrifying thing for a self-proclaimed Nothing to be, since now even the least little being spoils your spread.—Valéry, I think, makes the Serpent speak of the stain of Being on the whiteout of his domain.

Some folks just know that if you don't like something they go for it's because you don't "get it." What if it's because you do?

People engage not so much in self-deception as in self-avoidance; they don't fool but displace themselves.

32   SIN

That evil can be fascinating is world-scandal number one; that philosophical contrivances can be intellectually involving is an only slightly narrower outrage, namely insofar as willful badness is somewhat worse than deliberate sophistry. But who are we, that perverse desire and headstrong intelligence thrill us? Saving grace: not for long. (Here I am, writing "we," when I've foresworn that specious first person plural for imputations of fault—though, to be sure, I'd sooner use it of *all* my fellow-humans in a bunch than in its familiar restricted application: "We Americans . . .")

It's a this-worldly half-wisdom that "no good deed goes unpunished." Well, 1. surely not "no" good deed, and 2. a lot of good deeds being ill-considered, some disciplining of the do-gooding tic, administered by way of ingratitude, is, as they say, "appropriate."

So it's also half-true, and for the above good reason: most helpfulness means involvement, and that's often unwelcome. Here's the lesson: If you don't want effect B, don't be its cause A.

As they used to say where I come from: "Nu, what else is new?" (Brooklyn, way back.)

All told, my sins of omission far outweigh (do they weigh at all?) my sins of commission. Omissions are tainted nothings, and even my sins of commission are offenses nothing as rank as King Claudius's,* probably because I lack the resources. Moreover, I don't feel guilt-laden.—Then why do I remember so well and so often? Perhaps my conscience got divorced from me, but still lives down the block, a neighbor appearing rarely but not easily turned off. Funny, all in all I'm not for living a comparative life (which Plutarch made his people do; sensible readers concentrate on one of the pair). But in this case it's a comfort to be statistically integrated: about at the median, midway between the best and the worst.

Anyhow, this is my hyper-practical way with my conscience: Fix it and/or forget it. So far I've never—no, hardly ever—been backed into a rift I couldn't leap over or been faced with an abyss I couldn't back away from, never been mortally tried in a large way, except in my imagination. Is it fate's favor or disdain?

* "O, my offense is rank, it smells to Heaven" (*Hamlet*).

I have, without rejecting, thus guiltily, transgressed to varying degrees most of the Ten Commandments* applicable to me, but the second one I just don't accept, and so I breach it innocently, a pagan born of a Jewish mother: I find myself having happy truck with imageable gods and gladly gaining entrance into imagined worlds. And so I resist the jealous injunction of a divinity to relinquish his gift, that of image-viewing and making. For He, who is said to have made us in His image, must, therefore, have had that power Himself, and thus must have similarly endowed us, His image. Bluntly: this God doesn't have the right to forbid image-making.

In short: Images *per se* haven't even a whiff of sin about them, though there are surely culpable imaginings and evil images—culpable and evil because of the intention and the content, but not because of our very capacity to make second worlds. The first world, it is repeatedly said, seemed good to its Maker, so why shouldn't it be replicated, extended, enhanced? As to the chief worry, that man-made images can be used for idolatry, that's not a strong argument against human image-making, because God's own, the first world, is already replete with beings that can be, and have been, idolized, including stones.

Exodus.

Is being wrong the seamy side of being right or rather an exergue, an obverse, the respectable hindside of truth? Why is there usually a queasiness to being right, or worse, "in the right"? Not only because the opponent's self-respect is then my responsibility, but also because the fact that my triumph depended on his defeat intimates that his side had its potency.

Not to speak of the further fact that opposing otherness is a hundred-headed hydra.

Naiveté: the blessed wisdom that arises from ignorance of badness; really sensible people are often child-like—because prudence, pro-vidence, the foresight of anti-forces, isn't quite the virtue political-philosophy types think it is.

Sometimes the blessed spontaneity of obtuse simplicity is what's wanted.* Yes, but when?

*Example: Captain Delano of Melville's *Benito Cereno*, who forfends harm by his blind innocence.

Good persons can do bad things and still be good for a time, but then, one day, they're just bad.

A sad truth: I'm overtly nice to others to atone for too often being not-so-nice to them within. What about bringing the two realms into conjunction, on the friendly side?

"Doing the right thing": bulling through your own opinion.

We owe this interpretational generosity* to our own and others' humanity: to take who we mean to be as a substantial factor in who we are. For example, having mean impulses and suppressing them is to be imputed to us for virtue. That's a *very* un-Christian† denial of *sinfulness*, a propensity, as opposed to a *sin*, an actuality.

*I'm thinking of the hermeneutic (interpretational) principle of charity: "Impute maximum meaning to the text."
† Or, at least, un-Protestant.

To be wanted makes me far more inclined to be helpful than to be needed—such is human (my) perversity.

More on perversity: I'm told: "Take all the time you want," and I do it right away. I'm bidden to have it done in three days, and I can't get going: the stutter of constraint.

We shouldn't drive people into a most wrongheaded arrogation of guilt—that of their people or their parents—when the very notion of a fungible or transferable blame is poisonous. The wrongs of yesteryear cannot be on the heads of the not-yet-born.* People in our democracy *can* be fairly said to collude in the wrong of their generation, but even that has its limits: *injuriae multae, vita brevis.*

* *Pace Numbers*, which says that the Lord visits "the iniquity of the fathers upon the children into the third and fourth generation" (14, 18); *that's* iniquitous.

Sin just enough to get bored with it, sin in youth to free up your adult life for better things. Or you can work it inversely. Be a good person and compensate with a whopping mid-life crisis.—But seriously: *when* in life you commit your dedicated budget of bad deeds will shape your life's course. In any case, be sure to arrive in old age tired (that's unavoidable) but not weary (of it all).

Secular original sin, well known to us all: the sense of being ineradicably in the wrong, aboriginally clumsy, congenitally blind, never knowing what we're really doing. However—that can be cast as debilitating self-doubt or as cheerful realism: Carry on, for all that!

According to the Christians we're bad to the dregs *and* of infinite worth—maybe even the latter *because* of the former. Go figure.

Well, I've figured, looked up the parables of the Lost Sheep Found and of the Prodigal Son Returned. *Plain perverse*, and the plaint of the frugal stay-at-home son has my sympathy: All these years I've served you obediently and never got so much as a little goat, and now this wastrel gets a fatted calf just for coming back!*

There's a soberly secular counter-saying—"the squeaky wheel gets the grease"—that makes sense to me: The bad ones make commotions that solicit and receive extra attention. No hallelujahs—just practicality.

* *Luke* 15 : 29–30.

Is it: Goodness must wage a losing fight for its place in this world?, or: Goodness will find a place reserved for it by this world? To go by the news, it depends on the day of the week.

A short story plot: The devil offers me a wish. I choose: "As many dollars as there are leaves on my willow oak." "Done," he says, "Now you count them, and if you're even one off, it's down to hell you go." I say, "Stupid devil, why don't you count them, since you'll have to anyhow, to check me out and claim my soul."

Why haven't I ever *met* an evil person (though I've been contemporaneous with several)? "Evil isn't what one does, it's something one is that infects everything one does."* Such beings, made in the image of the Devil, are rare; the energy to be evil is equal to that of being good, says Davies' character, while the rewards are negative, as I imagine. Then, if your very existence is evil, the only way to stop being a living badness is to leave life, to exit existence. But suicide itself is the ultimate sin, at least for those theologically involved, as the bad I've read of tend to be. So they, in their Natural Depravity,† perversely try to slough off their evil being by committing this final sin—a small class with a high mortality.

P.S. If evil is a way of being, it's congenital. Yet, is an evil infant even imaginable? Yes, in odd moments: original sin not as the disposition of an adult's soul but as an inherited incarnation in a baby's body. But this kind of thing doesn't happen in my backyard; it eventuates somewhere else, on the world-scene or in movies: "The Bad Seed" (1956).

* Robertson Davies, *The Rebel Angels*.
† Said of Claggart, the devilish master-at-arms, in Melville's *Billy Budd, Sailor*, who *might* be seen as stage-managing his own demise, bringing down goodness incarnate with it.

I owe something to my vices. They're mostly the sort to function as the security squad for sound self-love.

Don't even try to gobble up the global apple of discord and sin. But be an inside-munching worm: do small work for large purposes. As they say "Make haste slowly," so "Do great things minutely."

Admiration, worse, adoration from another, has a predatory aspect: It watches, seizes, ingests. It is a security camera trained on oneself only. To make it worse, there is always the sense that one asked for it, is culpable: You wished to shine and now you're caught in the reflected glare.

It's an even greater shame to be humanly wrong unknowingly than maliciously. (A gentleman—here's an infamous, dated and wholly plausible, definition—is a man who never insults anyone except intentionally.) That is because in human affairs alert acuteness must perforce precede reliable goodness. Socrates speaks of the failure of such antecedent knowledge as the "lie in the soul," implying that unconscious error is particularly culpable. Why? Because we're supposed to be comprehensively aware, self-aware and world-aware. The rest will follow—more or less.

Is "insecurity" an affliction or a flaw? In adults, the latter.

The concern for "the future of humankind" seems to me so supererogatory an anxiety, so vacuous a grandiosity, as to verge on the irresponsible. Are we, a creepy, crawly swarm, all going together to perdition? Worry locally (or at most nationally), where you can do some good.

I'm no animal lover. What am I to think of that dog who lived with and was clearly attached to my friend Vanni for years and years and never learned a word of English, like a Sicilian immigrant *nonna*? It's the abrupt discontinuities of ability (discounting the laborious little successes of animal ethnologists in proving us continuous with other primates) that make me stand-offish. And here's the ultimate un-ease: These essentially dumb beings seem to be affectively not unlike us; they develop particular love.* Though my friend Ray, a dog evolutionist, lover, and breeder, who should know, says: Don't you believe it; they're out for what they can get from us.

*I find that I've often used "particular" to modify attachments. I got that from reading the literature of monastic communities, where "particular friendships" are proscribed. The adjective captures the edginess of pin-pointed passion.

It's no virtue to forgive and forget wrongs easily since, from sheer disengagement, it burdens the world with an unrestored imbalance. But to forgive and not to forget is a vice, stemming from overextended generosity.

There are fearsome moments when the moral air is sucked out of your life-bubble, and you choke in a value-vacuum. It's when you're auditing your account book of deeds done and discover your debts.

We've been in free fall since Eve, the mother of us all, ate the apple of excitation. Will we hit rock bottom? The truth is it's an infinite way down, and we're always *in medias res*. Actually we don't fall deeper, we morph our modes of fallenness and fall more sophisticatedly.

33 SOUL

The soul's art: to transmute impetuous accesses of love into delicate acts of tact.

Decisiveness is a soul's elegance and dithering its galumphing.

This, at least, is not such a perplexity as it might seem: human interiors are impenetrable, yet the human soul is knowable. The first goes to the ever-changing *now* of our feeling and thinking, the second to the stable *always* of our human constitution: variable particularity—stable commonality. *Nota bene*: "variable" doesn't mean continually "new"; inner life (if I'm to go by myself—and novels) is very repetitive. And "stable" doesn't mean "invariant." Except in its ultimate reaches, in our essence, our Humanity Itself, our earthly nature comes in many types, and these in a multitude of individuals.

A sedate sensibility is a good complement for an adventurous intellect. Extremely acute senses tend to induce blunted thinking.

My guess: the nicest person has a spot of mildew on his soul and the really bad 'un a shoot of nobility trying to sprout within.

The soul has, as everyone knows, its psychophysics, its psychohydraulics. It can be stretched past its elasticity to what feels like a point of no return, or drawn down past its low-water level to apparently permanent desiccation. Nonetheless, the possessor of an overwrought psyche regards its affliction as being of the spirit, a dark night of the soul, a revelation of reality. Take a sleeping pill, if you must, or eat a bag of M&M's (seminar pills, they're for me). Be shamefully inconsistent for the nonce: a mind-body identity opportunist.

When does enthrallment morph into obsession? When you *can't* let go? When it *hurts*? But these are also marks of being devotedly at work, without and within. Here's my distinction: Clarifying internal disorder and clearing up external business, the latter for the sake of the former, are rightly compelling interests. They turn into compulsions when thinking and doing is driven by a fierce *need* to discharge psychic *pressure* rather than by an ardent *interest* in doing well by a *matter*, be it thought or action.

Ideological possession: the totalitarian takeover of the soul.

Perhaps the opacity of the embodied soul is a blessing. If we could dive right in, we'd be faced with a slew of brute mechanisms and terminal enigmas. As it is, through the screen of flesh, we get the selected good bits of communicable inwardness.

Austere natures have a peculiar sweetness, and maudlin ones a typical fetor.

Why is distance still such an indifference-multiplier, in spite of cyber-connectivity? Because we've not yet ceased to be tethered to bodies, and distance nullifies physicality. And because we've not yet stopped being attached to each other one by one, while distance abrogates unique intimacy.

The opposite of "distant" is "close." Both adjectives *seem* to be literally spatial and only metaphorically psychical. Yet, while we're still *embodied souls*, the metaphors retain a literal residue—the soul is space-involved. Everyone knows that; it's trivial. Nobody can explain it; it's a mystery.

Again and again: "Insecurity" is of the devil, not the grand Satan but the little Mephistopheles. It's a small vice, this deficiency of sang-froid, ratcheted into an affliction, the kind which that horrible *Diagnostic and Statistical Manual of Mental Disorders* probably certifies as insurance-covered—an egotism that demands sympathy to boot. The cure is in the Delphic "Know Thyself," supplemented by the practical application: "And then be what you've learned you are, a little inferior."* Old cartoon, analyst to patient on couch: "Well, maybe you *are* inferior." It's our common condition, that realistic "inferiority complex," and there's much comfort in accepting it.

*Or as Garrison Keillor puts it, thinking positively, of the Lake Wobegon children who are *all* "above average."

Skewering wit issues from a lacerated, sweet wit from an intact soul. But the loving humor of the *observant* soul seizes on felicitous collusions of the common language

(English, above all) and the uwitting comicality of others' humanity to bring forth *reverence in the elegant mode*, Jane Austen's very own fashion.

The soul has its electric fence that starts sparking, its Maginot Line that starts firing, when border intrusions are detected. Actually, the intimate, inviolable land is a small duchy on the psychic continent, and light-footed, unarmed border-crossings would be easy enough; usually they're casual and spontaneous. The guarded territory is small if densely populated—lightly accoutered visitors not unwelcome. But why expend myself in these European similes? Americans are especially good at observing the boundaries of smooth social intercourse—excepting the intrusive types with their battery of ludicrously crude psychobabble. But they're deaf by training and dumb by choice.

There's always one thing more to be said about the soul's conservatism, at least mine:

1. The actual over the possible, *pace* Heidegger, who's making me nervous as no other author I've studied with our students (2014 and 2015): The more I understand the less I trust.*
2. Speed only for busy-ness, slowness for being.
3. My numismatics professor's unforgettable wisdom: sound principles, corrupt administration—the mantra of my deanship.
4. Suspect—no, resist—goal-less change, the *Economist*'s destructive mantras: "Change or decline" and "Welcome constructive destruction."
5. Agonize *before* judgment, *then* enforce it without bleeding all over everything.

6. Love your own best, but don't disown the other; keep in mind ontology's practical teaching: Your own circle becomes your world by the concavity of its circumference, but it can't be a cosmos without its convexity, its periphery, its outside definition.

7. Use imagination
   to fore-see plausibly,
   to empathize selectively,
   to daydream vigorously.

8. Relish paradoxes but recall that they are supportable only because they *are*, in *some* manner, resoluble, composable, or supersedable (when you get around to it). Terminal paradoxes tend to tragedy, and tragedy is a taste I never acquired.

9. Enjoy local good without forgetting the global worst—but *don't* pretend a care if you have it not.

10. Start grossly, zero in patiently, refine at the end. That's my favorite mode: *staged futzing.*

11. Security check: "Your thought-package may be opened for examination or destroyed,"† *i.e.*, examine ideology philosophically, that is, subject thought that's packed it in with thinking that's alive and kicking.

12. Think hierarchically: reverence plus discrimination (in the old sense: well-judged distinction-making).

And so: don't let good words go out of use, don't leave language in the lurch by retreating before the language-rectifiers. But also develop an ear for great neologisms: my favorite from long ago and of Yiddish derivation: *glitch*, the slithering out of control of an intentional structure.

*Trust in a philosopher is way different from belief—the former goes to intellectual virtue, the latter to truth-telling.

Husserl is utterly veracious but not altogether persuasive. Untrustworthy but true doesn't happen—in philosophy. It can in fiction, where great faking *is* sometimes verity.

† Part of the airport security litany.

Self-confidence: No sensible person could have much of it. (They used to say: "If you're not in a panic you haven't grasped the situation"). Here's what one—I—should have a lot of: the confidence in devoted futzing, in undeterred barging ahead and consequent catch-up and the courage of having properly appropriated my limits and defects.

Modes of self-consciousness: cramped self-regard, cool self-observation, serene self-enjoyment.

Self-interest rightly understood,* the *acceptable* egoism, is—what else?—thought to require that understanding be applied to interest. But hold it: first to *self,* and that is no longer calculating rationality but speculative intellect. Low "Figure your *true* interest" implies a prior high "Know thyself."

* Tocqueville's phrase.

To live *sub specie et aeternitatis et saeculorum,* under the aspect *both* of eternity *and* of our times: what a shuttling trick!

Some souls are always on anxious standby, pager on; others live in sincere expectancy of a call; they're the more comfortable company.

Having it both ways: to live somatically in the science-secured present and spiritually in the wisdom-guarded past. Why not, really?

Artificial highs are the cul-de-sac of internality, as pure feels are its black-out.

Let's, just this one time, go terminally overboard: the soul is a galleon under full sail, lying too deep in the water with a burden of casks, laboring on under a gallant skipper searching out a harbor of refuge. No sooner warped in than the crew, not waiting for orders, off-loads: The harbor is a receptive friendship; the burden, casks of tears; the skipper, a vestige of self-control.

Suspended between infinite and infinitesimal—the human position that so appalls Pascal. Why? Where would we want to be but *in medias res*? *Homo sapiens recte interest*—amidst what there is, that's the proper location of interest. (Why am I talking Latin? Pinched *gravitas*.*)

*Re pinching, as some official said of the Elgin marbles, the Parthenon Frieze in the British Museum, which the Greeks want back: "Why should we return them; we stole them fair and square." (An unnecessarily self-incriminating concession, since there was no Greece to steal them from when Lord Elgin rescued them from the Turks, 1801–1812.) The conservationist in me has some sympathy for protective linguistic pinching and cultural stealing "fair and square." It bears a relation to learning from books.

The mysterious mutuality: The soul is modeled by its clay, the flesh; the body is informed by its foil, the soul.

I might consider selling my soul for a benefit, say wisdom, but not for a profit, say advancement. But, of course, who'd I be selling it to? An angelic shyster who would cleverly dispute the category.

There's a terrible tenacity in terminally tentative souls—no breakthroughs, which are the soul's caving in to the beneficent pressure of likelihood.

Undoubtedly all humans have souls. But pig out on weekend TV and it will seem that not all souls make it to the surface: celebrity faces.

Brain-storming, brain-washing, brain-anything: they've got the wrong organ.

Of course I don't subscribe to the idiotic notion that thinking and imagining and feeling *are* brain activities. I've seen pictures of the brain functioning but never of a thought being thought. Nonetheless, I am persuaded that the consciousness of terrestrial humans needs a sub-servient, non-lesioned brain, and to have the gift of such a brain entails a duty: Don't risk alteration by potent sub-stances. For that, so I think, is inverting nature: The soul is supposed to incite the body, not the converse. Recre-ation? Experimenting? What uncandid euphemisms! Why should refreshment need alien substances, and what protocols of discovery, what criteria of falsification do these researches obey? Here's an exception: as relief from the indignity of chronic pain.

Answer (not for public consumption) to a reductive materialist: You have a brain, I have a mind; you deny yourself a soul, I claim one. To each his (or as PC-minded editors emend: her) own, since it's a matter of preference (as you're apt to argue in other contexts).

Nothing vacates the soul like celebrity, the ultimate externalization.

Ultimate complexity prevents subtlety, since shadings cannot show up on composite ground. A complicated character might be cunningly ambiguous but isn't apt to be wisely deep. Naiveté forever!

34   SURFACE

The teachers I trust* think that the surface—appearance—is *at once* an entangling veil of, and a necessary way to, the depths of being. That specifically human surface, the face, is the prime instance of this duplicity; hence the reading of faces is a "propaedeutic," a pre-training, for philosophers.

*Socrates and his progeny. One may sophisticate this perplexing *duality* into a doctrinal *confusion* of ontology and phenomenology, the accounts of Being and of Appearances (Heidegger, *Being and Time*, p. 30).

Can we read faces? Crude, brutish superficies can belong to delicate natures, and then again, it can be just as it looks. Delicately hued beauty, refined armatures can be the seat of human nonentity, or worse, negativity. So, no, we can't. Or better, by the time we can read truth in a face, we've already learned it from the other sources, from what's been said and done.

Yet blank peering isn't in us; we try to interpret the moment we look. And sometimes first sight—there may begin a life's tale.

Who thinks of the face they wear but don't see? Consider: you've never beheld your face in the flesh. Even the public, who *can* see it, rarely looks. Whence come those mirror-moments when this visage seems simply oddly slapped on: Why just this persona (a false etymology—they're the best ones: *per-sona*, "what sounds come through," a speaking mask)? Here's what it is: My face, never to be seen by me *in propia persona*, is said to, probably somehow does, bear the stamp of my *person*, this "undividable" individuum, this "uncuttable" atom. But my *self*, my soul, is not a person but a huge quasi-spatial expanse, stuffed with soul-furniture, opening into shifting landscapes under ever-changing emotional skies, and in no finite ratio to that 8"×6" patch of few features, my face. This visage is simply inadequate as a façade for our internal life. Two trailing blessings, really one: our body is the natural screen of our soul, an uncircumventable privacy-protector *and* thereby an incontrovertible proof-provider of our dual nature, body without, soul within.

These are spatial metaphors introspectively experienced; whoever discovered their tenor* would have found what it is to be human.

*The *tenor*, "holder," of a metaphor is the reference to which the *vehicle*, "carrier," is likened. Here the search would be for the real reference of psychic internality, which is likened to the spatial relation of insideness. In brief, what makes us speak of the soul, be it mind or imagination or affect, as *within* our body?

No one knows how this works, how the sensory surface turns into testimony of psychic depth. Self-certified interpreters of somatic signs are charlatans. Read research on facial expressions (Darwin wrote the classic) and despair: No one can explain why "down-in-the-mouth" is the look of being "sick-at-heart."

What a remarkable apprehension, one of those that come on you and go so fugitively that you can hardly recall what it was that startled you: Other people, of whom I am only thinking, are *there*, somewhere present to themselves, though not to me, really and truly independent of me and, by that very fact, really there for me from time to time, that is, when we're in the same place.

The demonstration of righteous anger is deliciously exhilarating to its entertainer but embarrassingly deflating to its drafted audience. Who wants to watch impassioned moral performances? Well, actually . . .

For some types, inherently ludicrous beings, the proper idealization is the cartoon. Are humans among them? Are even manatees bizarre in their essence? Perish the thought!

They praise portrait painters for putting in the warts, but lovers will think the mole's a beauty-spot. So surface is ambivalent. What about soul? Is a little black stain similarly duplicitously attractive?

Our constitutional disproportion: Here's that small facade, our face, more or less fixed, though perhaps bright-eyed one day and grungy-complexioned another, open-visaged now, then forbiddingly closed, but always that small, pre-modeled surface which it is for us to inscribe but for others to read. And then, behind it, there are the "innumerable fields and grottoes and caves" of imaginative memory* which are partly the world's, partly ours to shape and furnish, fields limitless in extent. And beyond even that expanse the thinking soul: "You could not discover the limits of the soul if you traveled every road to do so—such is the depth of the *logos*."†

* Augustine, *Confessions*, Book 10, the finest phenomenology of the internal landscape I know.
† Heraclitus.

How do we come to discern each other's inner life on such spare external evidence? Where there's interest, we are good exegetes of minimal texts.

The enigma of the human façade, the face: Is it a result or a cause? Well, the stuff and its structure, "porridge features" or "good bones," are our given lot. But then there's a life led and a soul evinced. The base and its feasibilities may be from nature, the mobility and its traces are surely ours. Best proof is the *belle laide* (in English the reverse, "the ugly beauty"), in whom an ill-featured face has a lovely animation.

35   TEACHING

Teacher's heed: not observation, as of an assessable specimen, but attention, as of an interesting person.

Recently saw a young man, one of ours, three women in tow, wearing a large black beaver hat with a collection of Soviet memorabilia pinned on, red star, hammer-and-sickle, *et cetera*. Says he to me, who has raised an eyebrow: "I want to irritate both extremes—animal rights types and conservatives." Well, thought I, that's one way to achieve that vaunted mean, declared the essence of virtue by Aristotle.

Walked by a Santa Fe transfer: "You look like Eva Brann." I said: "There's a reason for that." Student looked first befuddled, then pleased. I love walking on campus.

A teacher obstinately takes students disposed to be unserious seriously until they live up to it. Something similar sometimes works for dispositions: meet gracelessness with so much indefeasible niceness that it buckles and breaks up—snowed, as they say.

One task of a teacher: by a more comprehensive *and* minute attention to students' utterance than they themselves can give it (being entangled in the utterance itself), to interest them in themselves as thinking beings—their natural focus being their affective natures, or why would they tend to say "I feel that . . ." when what's required is "I think that . . ."?

Those students seem to me most admirable who are captivated by admiration, even adoration—who know what it is to lack and long, quail and emulate—to feel the exultation of being the lesser, bound by love to a greater, the pride of recognizing superiority, the generosity of pure delight in it. You have to be young; with maturity comes a more distant, more mordant view of even of the finest of fellow humans. Yet, if moments of being simply overcome by some magnificence or other have ceased altogether, you're not so much old as wizened.

Our students often know more than they know how to say. Life passes, and it's the other way around.

Students feel obliged to become hyperbolic in their paper-writing analyses of poetry.* They profess terrors, upheavals, weepings.—Doesn't happen. Perhaps a frisson, a shudder, a solitary tear. And yet, the truer, if more muted, movements are long-lasting, even life-shaping, perhaps not continuous but rather continual experiences, not vehemently upfront but insidiously backstage. To help these self-conscious, emotive responses to the arts settle into the quietly resilient descants to dailiness—that's our civilizing function.

*Not so a young officer from our naval neighbor in my graduate poetry tutorial: He used to sit with his chair on its hind legs, tilted back from our conversation, and proudly professe to have no access to the stuff. One day he keeled over backwards, and when he came back up, unhurt, he pulled his chair to the table and had access. In military men shame works wonders. He was *very* good.

I thought my advisee was a little yokelish, until I got a note: He wants to meet "before our solsticial adjournment." It took me a moment: spring vacation. Did Mencken say something to the effect that no one ever lost money over-estimating American witlessness? Wrong-headed!

Insight from Marx (read for Senior Seminar), who turns out to have foreseen everything (Existentialism, Pragmatism), everything, that is, but actual events: For example, come the Revolution, sweaty labor will be abolished in favor of refreshing work, while remuneration will have no reckonable relation to proficiency. However, it *is* that way now for real teachers—intrinsically rewarding work for which the salary is necessarily modest, but the reward from students is often undeservedly munificent: long-term gratitude for having once been let loose on learning, sometimes half a century delayed. But gratitude is, unlike justice,* the later in coming, the sweeter.

* "Justice delayed is justice denied," a legal maxim with a long history.

It's a teacher's labor to undo all the humanistically deformed trickle-down from physics and mathematics: complementarity, uncertainty, duality, relativity, probability, and incompleteness, not to speak of terms intruding from other systems, as the one I heard a student call the "Zeetgeest."* Would that there was a forfending formula that people—especially at conferences—were required to chant before they speak: "I will try my darndest to abstain from mis-employing a scientific term to construct specious analogies, and, should I be sure of my artifice, I will be responsible for supplying, in three minutes, a credible understanding of the borrowed science."

* Hegel's *Zeitgeist*.

Inhibition, insecurity, introversion—illnesses, I could bet, in that insufferable *DSM* (the psychiatrists' bible)—must, in truth, be vices, or why would they be so off-putting? One of my legendary Russian-Jewish colleagues proposed this emendation to our Program so that it might better respond to students' self-exculpatory descriptions of their derelictions: First year: Plato with whippings; second year: Bible *sans* whippings. If that's what he actually said, were they to be whipped *out of* or *into* reading philosophy? And were they to think better of the Hebrew Bible for not being worth a drubbing, presumably administered by the much-beloved Mr. Kaplan? Anyhow, word-lashings over therapy-referral anytime, as a first option.

In institutions of higher education, "doing my own work" does not mean helping students learn. Not here.

Students need to hear that these adolescent torments will turn into mature interests, less anguishing but just as gripping. Young fixations are sublimated, distilled, into engaged inquiries. Liberal learning is the alembic.

"Can't" often means "won't"; it's a teacher's talent to tell when.

Musil's "The Perfecting of a Love," the students' choice for an all-college seminar: forty pages of micro-psychology, nano-sensibility. That was the torture of adolescence—having to bring to adequate articulation the mini-movements of consciousness. What a relief the grosser psychic life of maturity is, with its practical problems and immediate responsibilities! Musil got stuck.

The generations of students, be they boomer, greats, X's, seem to me not so different, having (for the time being, at least) all been born as human babies. Perhaps here's a difference. It used to be possible to tell the innocent from the experienced; now it's practically impossible—and hard to tell whether they themselves make a distinction—being way ahead of their own real lives, born within the virtual world and given to gravityless "experimentation."

The problem that our most in-love-with-learning students must solve once outside: how to come down to earth without landing in quicksands. Or: how to be practical in continuity with theory, rather than by breaking away from it. Or: how to let their learning become operative.

Don't preach freedom to students, they'll take it as an incitement to rebellion. Ask what it is, how it relates to fulfillment, and in what mode it's desirable.—As an "in-itself," freedom is first exhilarating, then tedious, finally malaise-making. As a "for-something," it's the prelude to fixated effort and so, the condition of work. As such it has as many modes as there are hindrances to one's powers—modes internal (distraction, incapacity, monomania) and external (conformism, indigence, tyranny).

Though I'm much for immediacy in teaching and learning—putting no pretensions of office between tutor and student and no introductory matter between book and reader—there's much to be said for those secular intercessors, the holy ghosts of worldly life: the laws of nature between God and man, constitutions between rulers and ruled, civic society between government and private citizens.*

*And Tocqueville says it.

Passionate resistance spells imminent conversion; that includes the struggle against the trammels of learning.

To freshmen Socrates first shows himself as a rationalistic bully. Often enough those who feel most offended fall the hardest, once they've divined what he's up to: Few of them, though the offspring of good parents and the pupils of devoted teachers, have ever been taken so *completely seriously* before.

Student on a self-involved reader: "He spits on the page and looks at himself in the bubbles."

Young dignity, once again, is moving, and teachers expend themselves according it more recognition than its subject's deportment, raiment, and grooming would seem to warrant.

Definition of fame: More people have heard of you than you've heard of. Every teacher is famous: known to parents, siblings, high school friends. On Parents' Day: "I've heard so much about you." Here's a human propensity, perhaps a saving grace: We're always looking at our students, appreciatively, critically, sometimes even attractedly, repelledly. But we don't often think that they're looking at us even more intently, we being few, they many. So now that I *am* thinking of it: the less I know, the better—and that for better and worse.

Gnomic speech: students demand its expansion, rightfully expecting brief speech to bear long meaning. It's a kind of trust—as I trusted (profitably, I think) Heraclitus, for example. So trust justifies succinctness. Prolixity, then, by contrast, is a right accorded to the ideationally challenged.

Of all the educationist blather, this is, to me, the most vapid: You have to be where the students are. Then what good are you to them? Here's the sensible version: Discern where they are and start way ahead.

What is so affecting in students is the way their inevitable stereotypicality masks their natural peculiarity; they look like specimens of their generation, but they long like no one but their utter selves.

Not said to students quite like this: You've large capacities which you've filled up with yourself. Practice *kenosis**
and be full of the world.

*Greek, "emptying" in theology, relinquishing godhead to become man.

Watch the news: The human race is in decline. Teach the young: Humanity gets more wonderful by the year—an absolutely plausible paradox.

A liberal education is the most effective boredom-preventative (outside all those discretionary activities dangerous to life and limb) known to me. And since boredom is the most explosive mental condition known to civilization (as inexpressiveness is to private life, also cured by such education), liberal education is man's greatest good, without hyperbole.

Freshmen in the "Awesome" mode, bestowing a semi-deserved compliment: whether to slurp it up or spew it out? Surely not the latter, but not the former either. Appreciate not only the particular intention (generosity toward me) but the larger ability to admire (a great virtue in general), but deprecate the flattery: "Stay with it for four years, and you'll know pretty much the basics of what I know."

I'm studying, facing works of the intellect: "I don't understand what it's saying." That may have two possible causes: 1. *I* don't get it or 2. *it* doesn't make sense. "Be *very* wary of concluding the latter." That's good straight advice to myself. But for certain students it needs modulation, because it seems to grind in their limitations, and that is pedagogically counterproductive—and not very nice.

After commencement: making the rounds of our new-coined *alumni*, "nurselings," who leave us now with as much glee (momentarily damped by nostalgia) as they once left their parents. First family: "He says you're the embodiment of the Program." I swell. Second family: "He says you're the college mascot." (*Nota bene*, the neighboring Navy's mascot is an old goat.*) I deflate. Well, that's being alive and breathing.

*I've told this twice. That's to honor life's witty collocations—and a sign of the senility that has been dogging me for some eighty years.

If you love to shed your footwear in class or other convocations, your feet probably feel like free spirits. But your neighbor feels a complementary respiratory inhibition. And so with all manner of free spirits.

Does "the less said, the better" about ticklish subjects always hold? Yes, probably, but I've found myself, I know not how, deep in conversation with a clueless kid, innocent of all that the academy calls "cultural literacy," but with so much good heart, acute perception, and unaffected interest that posing a pressing human problem to him (not mine, to be sure) was a veritable refreshment.

Last night (2014) my freshmen were discussing Aristotle, *Metaphysics* Lambda, on the Unmoved Mover who activates by attraction. I asked: Who provokes keener desire, the beloved who returns love or the unmoved, unregarding one? For once, snickering embarrassment! Was it that they, grand-children of the sexual revolution, just have no experience of the ardors of unreciprocated love (couldn't be, could it?), or was it that after half a century of sexual free speech, their natural shame is intact? Anyhow, they have to learn to speak of intellectual arousal, just as equivocal in fact as in word.

Sweet madness: Homecoming. Alumnus from my very first years, a promising mathematician but even then on the brink of mental illness, leaves messages from a noisy restaurant. "I'm in Annapolis, and I wanted to go to your seminar but I've lost my paper." No phone number left. Two days later from his home, in another state. "And I've got something interesting to tell you!" This time a number. I call him—he's bubbling over. The Holy Spirit came to him in a dream and promised to help him prove X's conjecture (something about complex numbers by a contemporary of Gauss). There's a million-dollar award for it, and if he wins it, he'll remember me. I wished him luck. He: "I don't need luck; I've got the Spirit." I quickly retract and credit the Intercessor. He forgives me; after all it's been well over half a century, and here we both are— from him a word torrent, but filled with confiding sweetness. In the good, madness can be lovable.

Sometimes, *sometimes*, it is possible to induce a smidgen of grace in the graceless by undeflectable niceness.

Vehement preconceptions are a world apart from firm opinions; that world between is opened by liberal learning.

36   TIME

Should life be taken as a streaming continuum or a punctuating discontinuity? Well, you want your physical being to be reliably continuous, but the soul relishes discontinuities—such as high and low, yes and no, here and beyond.

Time's an iffy anodyne; not all pains diminish, some become chronic. Better bet: do the next thing, and then the thing after that, and recur to hurts only when half a dozen things have been taken care of. Doesn't always work either, actually.

Sleep filches time from life, but it also extends it. Is that a good bargain, seeing the time is lost now and added later, when there may not be much life in the life-increment? On the other hand, even a month, even a diminished month, is in definite proportion to a life-time, hence to be reckoned with, while it is in an infinitesimal ratio to eternity, and so it is no reckonable loss at all to death-time.

The gauzy enchantment of time's curtain swathes the past of psychic memory, but the past of documentary memory is curtainless, mundanely bare, sharp-edged. Snapshots of seventy years ago—and it's a dry-eyed: "Oh yes, that was him, her, it," just as sentiment-less as yesterday's meeting with an acquaintance. Even one's near and dear are curiously unatmospheric in a photo-album. Imagine the bottomless indifference of current selfies and videos in a decade—if anything has survived.

There is a psychological analogue to the theological notion of the "standing now," the *nunc stans*, the perpetual moment of eternity. It is the so-called "specious present," the extended now, which is, like the standing now, a logical paradox. It is our time of actual being there. All the rest, all my eight and a half decades plus, are withdrawn, lost-time territory: *passed*, *past*, and are accessible only through the spontaneous offerings or laborious retrievals of memory. The lived "now" alone holds intimations of timelessness, passage-less actuality. But it *is* a self-contradiction—*both* extended *and* momentary.

P.S.: Apply your thinking imagination to a life lived continuously, a non-momentary, un-momentous life. Does any figure come to mind? Even our mathematical comprehension of a continuity focuses not on the envisioning of a gapless line-continuum but on the operation of cutting that always hits a point.* But neither does our cognitive imagination have a fine-grained way to represent continuities; they simply appear as statically or fluidly compact—grossly untrue to ongoing now-consciousness. In short, our intellect tells us that our lives are temporally and spatially continuous, missing no moments, but our awareness is ineradicably sporadic: from packed moment to moment, separated by vacant indifference.

* Dedekind, "Continuity and Irrational Numbers."

The historical route: Here we are and there they were, so the in-between must have been *the* way to get here. *Post hoc, propter hoc*—seems pretty much a non-sequitur; some other route could have brought us about with only inconsequential differences.

Hold it: *Are* there indifferent differences? Or is it as with facial charm? All but undetectable alterations can make all the difference, that famous butterfly effect of physics applied to love and history.

Read somewhere: "Historians in the past assumed that men learned from their previous mistakes." Damned right, they did—learn how to do it again.

Bacchai: "Whoever pursues great matters won't achieve the present (*ta paronta ouchi pheroi*)." Generally I find choral wisdom a little drivelly, but (in my version) Euripides here gets to me: You can foreclose your now by thinking big.

1. Living as spending time: Was it a *good* time?
2. Living as experiencing moments: Were they *significant* moments?

Vacations, vacated time, are said to be re-creations. Well, at a cost. "Being away" pushes the daily now into the past, and disrupts lived sempiternity, the endlessly recurrent as opposed to the "standing" now. Then, from this ungrounded state of suspension you have to re-connect your life—and no service to call.

"Multitasking," "quality time": if it has four syllables it isn't to be taken for idiocy but for efficiency.

Is the personal passage from a painful past to affect-purged history ever completed, once and for all?

Clocks evince the total irrationality of mechanisms: I'm at work. I look, it's 2 AM. I look again, it's 4:30. But why? No time passed! Solution: it's got nothing to do with clock-time.

I don't have to understand every enigma I meet; if I'm told that someone, somewhere has clued it out, I rest satisfied. Recently my curiosity was piqued by the question: Why do mirrors reverse reflections laterally but not longitudinally? (One of those obvious phenomena we just don't notice.) One and a half hours with my encyclopedia of mind, and now I know—or did for a day. Lesson: suppress curiosity (so beloved by reforming educationalists), and you'll gain time for the mysteries no one has comprehended. *That's* time profitably spent—it buys a bit of eternity.

"Reality" has its moments of poetry, but since it is a continuum, they are swallowed up, overwhelmed in the more-than-dense running-off that is the world's going. But if attention fixes such a glow-point and sends it into memory, it becomes a permanence, and the indifferent continuum has been blessedly interrupted—a point on it has irrupted:

> What is anyone? What is he not? The dream of a shadow
> Is man. *But* when comes a god-given gleam,
> A radiant ray rests on men and a honey-sweet moment.
> Pindar, Eighth Pythian

These are the only lines of his *Odes* I ever *really* understood, so I'll cite them twice, thrice, ever trying to get them right.

37   TRUTH

So it's pre-dawn time, and certain bare truths become salient. "Face it," courage calls. "Bury it," cravenness counters. Better have it out.

Suppose someone—God or Man—told us truths of which we could be indefeasibly certain, about life's end and its hereafter, about the actual venue of imagined beings, about our unavoidable obligations, so that we no longer lived in ignorance lit up by wild surmises—that would undermine our existence, meaning our temporal being. We'd be done and done for.

Clarity is the best we get in searching for truth—and even that's always premature. Here's the next thought: If there were not Truth (whether or not for us), nothing could be clear, neither a semi-final paradox, nor a delimiting negation, nor an intermediate conjecture. Where there's a way, there's a destination.

Could a well-trained historian ever take the oath to tell the truth, the whole truth, and nothing but the truth? "To tell the truth" he'd have to know it; "to tell nothing but the truth" he'd have to know untruth as well; but "to tell the whole truth" he'd have to be immortal.

The pursuit of Truth, an arduous activity with uncertain outcome, is certainly avoidable, "the world" being a huge system of respectable diversions: maintenance, productivity, recreation. Consequently, "The truth is great and will prevail / When none care whether it prevail or not"* is a proclamation either merely self-confirming (since it suggests that whatever prevails is truth), or pretty unwise (since it appears to obviate effort). Why am I underwhelmed by these discouraging facts? Because I rarely have recourse to "truth" in framing my questions to myself; I want to know what and how things *are* (both *pragmata*, "human affairs," and *res*, "thingly things"). Thus truth, with its moral intimations (since its opposite is falsity, both incorrect and deceptive), seems an unnecessary screening interposition between me and my objects.

* Coventry Patmore.

Catastrophically crestfallen: by the sudden deflation of a buoying faith. Don't do it to anybody! Demythification is a discretionary type of truth-telling, refrain-worthy.

Brilliance seizing truth—cry havoc!

Every sensible person is supererogatorily superstitious: A confident prediction needs to be countermanded by crossed fingers under the table, and even a hurried walker needs to avoid stepping on the cracks. Why leave anything to chance?

Speak truth to power and piss them off terminally, especially since it usually isn't all that true. Better helpfully reveal dangers and earn—ephemeral—gratitude.

Never think reactively, that is, motivated by the present and impending "situation." It makes for truth-deformation. Yet, how else? Go into the sleep-walking—I mean, efficient—mode that fits managing a situation,* and don't forget to wake yourself up when it's over. Then think it out.

* What in my deaning days I called "the Dean's Dormition."

Truth is in complexity—because the world is a tangle. / Truth is in simplicity—because the world is a tangle. So there are kinds of truth: looking-glass truth and through-the-looking-glass truth.

Here's what would make my day, nay, week. I'm a watcher of cooking shows. (It's a great trick to convert a seen dinner into an eaten one.) When they've plated the dish they hand it to their stand-by to taste, who throws her eyes to heaven and says "Yumm." Now if just once this stooge took a mouthful and said: "Yecch . . . !"

38 WORK

I'll take dilettantic futzing over professional functioning any time. Well, most of the time; there's a right moment for knowing precisely what's what: plumbers who fix the faucet and doctors who fix me. Even a bureaucrat sometimes fixes a foul-up (usually caused by same).

Busyness is an invidious type of laziness, one long avoidance maneuver to forestall leisure, the labor-free space for coming to terms with our doings: "A life of accomplishments"—good ones?

Can anyone be a good judge of practical realities who hasn't thought out impractical radicalities?

Marriage: the normalizing, universal, necessary institution for our social being. To be sure—but realized in the most modulated, particular, adventitious privacies of our beings. Otherwise put: I'm for it in general, but averse in particular.

P.S.: It's a boon to have been good-looking in youth: No one can assume it wasn't a choice. But who'll believe the flat truth? I've always liked work best.

Precipitating oneself into business-to-be-done is the most accessible—and chimerical—termination of inertia, because business is just surreptitious idleness, diversion from real work. Still, it's better than socked-in stagnation: "oblomovism."*

* After Oblomov, the titular hero of an epic novel by Goncharov (1859) about a man who wastes away from doing nothing, hardly ever leaving his divan. I've owned this Russian "*Iliad* of the dressing gown" for over half a century, but every time I try again, I get discouraged at its vastness. For a tautly sad *short* story of voluntary inanition, give me its taciturn American counterpart, Melville's "Bartleby the Scrivener."

People who live a practical life going places in a time-bound world rejoice in their day full of expectant ways and venues. The others who live a sessile contemplative life in an atemporal world—are their days full of serried satisfactions? No, they go to their proper activities reluctantly, even aversively, and spend much of their day in preparatory diversions; not for nothing does "leisure" mean both vacant time and recreational time (both sorts of "vacation"), more the former than the latter. The best of students can be compulsive time-wasters.* But there's a "but": Even a little time on a sober high goes a long way in making life good, and you learn to make regular work evolve its spontaneous moments.

* In Herman Hesse's *Nürnberger Reise* there is a charmingly shocking confession of the time-wasting, diversion-seeking, work-aversive indolence that afflicts members of the leisured professions, writers above all.

From our labors we get time off, and so we must from our world—even if we've lived, as we certainly don't, in a world of never-roiled dailiness, continually fulfilling work, and boredom-proof leisure, a world devoid of emergent threats and distant dangers. For as we expend ourselves in the particular exertions of our occupation, so we are worn away by the mere existence of our spatio-temporal being. To go on this existential (forgive me!) vacation we were given an internal quasi-world, the imagination, a place and a productive power of scenes, filled with activity we are permitted to control. And behold, time spent in this venue is not only a recreation for the soul but a rehearsal for worldly action: It is a setting for practicing literal *prudence* = providence = foresight. We preview scenarios and return world-ready.

Is work an anodyne, so effective as to occult the underlying pain of mere living? Read Dostoevsky or James novels in which no one visibly works and everyone is somewhat-to-very miserable. Add Marx (this week's seminar reading), who writes a lot of brilliant fiction, but seems to be right about this: Labor is onerous, but work is our species-nature. So it appears that work doesn't hide life's basic pain, but that its absence *is* that pain.* Being without *occupying* occupation is an insidious death—life-time being killed. Even labor is better. Our recession brought that home, quite aside from that basic "making a living," without which there is no making a life. Well, for a while there's bohemian sponging, but it's rarely compatible with a work in hand.

*As ever, William James: All that was real passes away, he says, but "more zestful than ever is the work, the work" (*Psychology*, Ch. XI).

How physical constitution tints one's truth: Socrates outlived a lusty youth into a naturally moderate maturity, could drink the company under the table, had a cast-iron stomach (which he enjoyed up to a limit), a skin like a pelt with soles like leather, and a kindly tolerance for his followers. So he's for wakeful sobriety and intellectual ecstasy. Nietzsche had a delicate stomach, high-strung nerves, an invalid's moderation and reclusive proclivities fraught with longing for followers. So he's for Dionysiac vitality and deflationary metaphysics. Guess whom I trust?

Philosophize from strength!

I'm an "everything-in-its-place" fanatic: given a lifetime's accumulation, culling which would be impious, putting things where they live is the only de-cluttering device available.

Two helps for tomorrow: stop before you're finished, though it be only 3:30 AM, and put all the books back on their shelves.

Best advice, from Yeats's "To a Friend Whose Work Has Come to Nothing": "Be secret and exult"—much better than licking wounds in public. Besides, if "nothing comes from nothing" is probably false, "nothing comes to nothing" is probably true.

They say that anything worth doing at all is worth doing well. But there's a competing truth: Anything worth doing at all is worth doing even badly—just so it gets done.

Whence distraction? The clutch of daily maintenance, the curse of secular perfectionism, the care of human obligations. And yet, I, we, were never wholly captured by the world to which we're self-bound—as music helps us recall.

Would that we were allowed to say so:* An *absolute* right to be or do something does not imply a necessity to do it, nor does a *de jure* right not to have something done to one constitute a *de facto* guarantee against it happening. In personal conduct, practicing prudence is better protection than relying on rights; it's the opposite in politics: principles over caution, within reason.

*It's called blaming the victim, and you do it, that is, caution people, at your peril.

Some people thrive on mess—or have a blessed obtuseness to it. Others, like myself, are environmentally distractible. There's an old cartoon: Man sitting in a deckchair expecting to relax, glances up at his house. And every venue—roof, rainspout, window sash, doorknob—has blown a little bubble: "Fix me!" So disorder, fix-soliciting, babbles at me. It's my Teutonic heritage and no virtue, but it's incurable; without this affliction I could have written three more books. So maybe it's a saving grace after all.

Money is fungible desire, goods are fixed choice. That's in normal life, but in financial trading it seems to be the reverse—eerie.

The trick: turn agonies into thought-projects, anxiety into work; convert debilitating dis-ease into exhilarating un-ease.

Life's business we do to be done with it; life's work we do to be doing it.

39   WRITING

Aphorisms: intended thought-vignettes, accidental quasi-poetry. Collections thereof: heaps of atomic idea-lets, webs of intimated coherence.

Can punctuated thinking reveal anything but an unmade-up mind? Yes, perhaps: the world's insuppress-ible unity.

Hippocrates wrote aphorisms. From a doctor I'd rather have prescriptions.

Two aphorists: Gracian (1647) and La Rochefoucauld (1678). Perhaps I'm basely denigrating my betters, but truth is, I'm not impressed:

La Rochefoucauld's last: "For a woman hell is old age." In my native language: *Quatsch*.

And: "The head is always fooled by the heart." *That* from a Frenchman? Always?

And: "In most men love of justice is only fear of suffer-ing injustice." Compare Hobbes: "Justice . . . is a rule of reason by which we are forbidden to do anything destruc-tive to our life." It's just as mordant but purged of flabby cynicism; Hobbes can render brute realism as taut wit: self-protection as rational righteousness!

And: "It is something less distressing to be deceived by the person one loves than to be understood." Illogical; if you're truly deceived, you're not at all distressed. And untrue to boot.

On Gracian's *Art of Worldly Wisdom* (*Prudencia*). This Spanish Polonius (translated, I wonder why, by Schopenhauer, whose own book teems with wiser worldly wisdom) has a terminally commonplace, small-gauged, not to say mean wisdom: some is just wrong, for example no. 299 of 300. I got that far by a personal adaptation of mathematical induction: No. 1 didn't quite work, and I suspected that for any n, n + 1 would do likewise; thus I didn't have to read them all to infer that the one before the last wouldn't be persuasive either. And behold, it wasn't: "Leave off hungry" (in the penultimate of three-hundred sayings that is assuming a lot). Indeed, I've long thought the opposite was true: Don't avoid surfeits of pleasure; they make you long for work. For surfeit is nature's conclusion, and desire, which is a natural resource, is most readily replenished when nature has rested satisfied. So, when you can, get really enough of what you crave, be it of meatloaf or social life.

And: "You can outsmart one other person, but not all others." Better put: "You can fool some of the people all the time and all the people some of the time, but you can't fool all the people all the time."*

Banal commonplaces, gussied up with worldly cynicism. I'll take Platon Karataev's† plain, round mantras anytime.

---

* Lincoln, quoted from memory, probably with loss of neatness.

† "Plato of the white pages," I've been told. He's the illiterate—I think—peasant sage at the center of Russian life in *War and Peace*.

"Confessedly literary works of aphoristic philosophy also flash light into our emotional life, and give us a fitful delight."—My hero,* especially when appreciatively disparaging: "Fitful," forsooth! "Delight," hear, hear!

Why "my hero"? Because, in his self-confident modesty, he anticipates, without origination-vaunting or movement-mongering, the practices and problems of several psycho-philosophical schools: 1. Phenomenology, in his robust discriminations and vivid descriptions of inner life; 2. Neurophilosophy, in his candid distinction between the determinist *predicate* proper to psychological science and the free-will *hypothesis* necessary to philosophical ethics; and 3. Philosophy itself, in pinpointing the small, crucial locus of the free self: our ability to summon interest and our power to maintain concentration—free will as attentional effort, the soul's "ownmost" (German: *eigentlichste*) capability, as it came to me a while ago.

*William James, *Psychology*, Ch. XXIV.

Why aphorisms? From Greek *aph-horizein*, "to delimit"—thus a thought so expressed as to be at once definite (just short of definitive) and, for a moment, self-explanatory, as of a mind in the pulsating mode. However—this is banal wisdom—though no sentence means in isolation, and no proposition proves by itself, yet any signifying compaction of words, like a magnet introduced among iron fillings, configures a field of contexts, complexities, qualifications. So aphorisms are deliberate discontinuities, gist-saving suppressions, extracted essay-vestiges. You might call them the stylites* of thought-devoted language.

Yet that's not quite right: They aren't only pruning-survivals but also compression-products, a sort of prosaic poetry: While the prosodic poetry of the lyre is artfully concise, the prosaic poetry of the pen is wittily abrupt.

I think the condition for producing aphorisms is *talent-lessness*: the urge to formulate in the absence of a gift for systematic coherence, for idea-plotting. Yet again, there's more to it: With the negative endowment comes positive *desirelessness* born of faith, reluctance to pull thinking together because coherence will supervene without my supervision. For the world, and most that's within it, *is*, and so it's somehow *one* (modified Parmenideanism).

*Ascetic Christians, each sitting on his pillar in the desert.

Paul says: "Do an aphorism on self-quotation." Fair enough; I'm up to perpetrating the deed. He means to be inciting wit, I tell him, but in fact he's inviting a disquisition. If I were quoting someone else's funny idea over the phone I'd get a smile; instead I hear a smirk. What is it with self-quotation?

Well, it's vanity, and vanity is not being able to get enough of yourself. Did anyone ever cite himself just once? You've rehearsed it, or you wouldn't be so ready with it. So self-quoting belongs to the family of iteration. Long ago, I read somewhere that if the brain has a pleasure center, it might be identical with a do-it-again center.

So there's a repetition-pleasure (spare cousin to the re-played daydream), seen in pecking animals and vain peo-ple. It's a pole apart from activity-pleasure, the "bloom" on being well at work.*

You've extruded, quite a while ago, a *bonbon-mot*, a long since inoperative thoughtlet encased in delectable language, like a cherry in chocolate. Now you can't get enough of what the Germans call an *Ohrenschmaus*, an "aural feast" (literally), a "musical treat" (by the diction-ary), and of the jolt of laughter it elicits from the snaffled audience.

Here's the voice of sobering sense—"Give me excess of it, that, surfeiting, / The appetite may sicken, and so die"†—but it doesn't work. Vanity is insatiable. So what's self-quotation? Self-pleasuring stuckness, verbally rehearsed.

* *Nicomachean Ethics.*
† *Twelfth Night.*

How is it that in strained moments, the mind is full of language debris, banalities that roll off a tongue struck with momentary vulgarity? Where did that come from? From the fact that adequate speech is a work of *discrimi-nation*, and under stress we become indiscriminate.

Good writing palpates and digs—poignancy and depth.

Like all my fellow-humans (except those afflicted with *logorrhea*, the verbal runs, in need of a word-cementing pill), I take down my utterance from my internal com-ment-stream by a factor of fifty. Of course, it's a matter of time—external time, which, being shared by all of us, is in much shorter supply than internal time. But that's not all. Tactful speaking-out curtails candor, which, when internal and uncensored, can be quite copious. Purposeful speech to the world had better get sooner and selectively to the point, around which, self-to-self, it meanders at unconstrained leisure. But above all, it's a matter of prideful caution: Inside I wield a memory-eraser, and misbegotten language, being non-utterance, simply disappears; outside what's said is said and stays said. Though, to be sure, people who talk long after they've finished saying something manage to make themselves unremembered even *viva voce*.

Go for verbal panache or linguistic dignity? Flip-flop.

A devoted scribbler is never terminally *aporetic* (at an impasse), since the pencil put to paper or the fingertips to keyboard can go off in an improvisation, an essay, a writing exercise, even when you've got nothing world-shaking to say.

A thought well-expressed is usually—don't I know it—an attenuated thought.

Think things out traipsingly and a resolving intuition will leap into your way, repudiating—deludedly—any connection to the slog.

When caught short, I'm blurting-honest—tell the truth without proper preparation; a crude simulacrum it turns out to be! Truth-telling on short notice is mere honesty, unguardedness; self-searching candor requires serenity. But even candid truth-telling has two meanings: saying what I am thinking and saying what is the case; they aren't the same very often. In fewer words: truth requires composed intention as the setting and actual knowledge as the substance. Final reduction: willingness *and* endowments.

Brevity is, they say, the soul of wit—and the cause of extensive commentary (example: the Torah, which contains the most concisely told stories I know).

People trying for significance tend to produce more gibberish than people just talking.

Stylistic grooming, the aim of rewriting, always transforms the first meaning. Is that honing or falsifying? Well, honing does concentrate significance, while falsifying transforms truth-values. So push the former as far as you can while indulging minimally in the latter.

Rule for English speech (not French): You can say anything as long as you know what rule you're breaking. It's one of those mystery effects, where knowledge modifies a situation just by lurking.

Another good word gone bad: "discrimination," from "acute judgment" to "invidious distinctions." To make up for it, bad words gone good: "Bad" itself in street talk, meaning "admirable." Is there another language like English for letting under-thoughts turn diction upside down?

One sort of repetitive wordiness happens when you say things that are easy to understand and hard to believe: "The proof is complete, / If only I've stated it thrice."*

*Carroll, *The Hunting of the Snark*.

Light-footed wit is a talent: linguistic leaping and an antic soul. Heavy-treading wisdom is an anti-talent: adequate expression and a sober mind. The former goes dreary well before the latter.

The capacity for high-class fun—in-jokes galore—is a bonus of being educated (liberally).

Apropos of nothing: looking into Gretchen's garden in Westport: Me: "Look, there's a goldfinch in the cosmos."* Barry: "Could you be more specific?" (Golden moment of linguistic wit.)

*For non-gardeners: a tall, annual, blowy flower; pink, lavender, many shades.

Some of these things I've said before, ten, twenty, thirty years ago: Is that reprehensible? Not on your life— in fact, it *is* my life—provided that it isn't just recitation from memory, literal recall, but yet another touching of the base, yet another rediscovery of the ground.

Why not have some trust in the Hermes* in us all, the common interpretive power that will get the intended gist if not all the thought of your communications? Therefore receive expressions of appreciation for things told with this faith: wherever an intensely personal experience is crossed with a broadly human reflection, people tend to resonate, if inexactly. So what if the echo is a little skewed? It wasn't, after all, a "repeat after me" session.

* The god Hermes, the messenger god, was the founder of hermeneutics, the art of interpretation.

Beware of being surprised into on-the-spot confidences—if you value the shapely accuracy of your expression. If you want to forestall misapprehension, write it out. Sometimes, however, a crude, somewhat deformed version of your sentiments does serve the occasion best—then babble away to meet the moment.

Does wit (the pride of Lycurgan Sparta) forestall wisdom (the prop of Solonic Athens)? Does concision abrogate reflection? Are aphorisms grasshopper thoughts? Better not go there.

Ideas: those who suffer from scarcity value their few highly and protect them fiercely. Those who teem with them are willing to regard some as throwaways; that's for the notions of the fore-mind*—who gives up deep-level thoughts without a fight?

* Pre-frontal cortex, if you must.

For writers to whom the human race is absurd (rather than mysterious), individual sin is no more: If the whole deserves a bitter laugh, no spot in it is particularly tainted.

Writing is an insistent urge that, unlike most urges, carries no obligation to control it—but being read is an extravagant desire that it would be wise to put down.

Re humor, here's the rule: the person with the less robust funny bone gets to say what's funny. It's hard to remember how variable are the humor-tunings, how movable the funny-bridges of the human instrument.

What is funny? My cowboy friends in Montana (they run a herd of a thousand, Black Angus) take every mishap from broken jaw to near-death as a joke; it's a point of honor—the ultimate cool. To me, funny is a live stereotype: men being male generically (to coin a term). That's perhaps the most gender-specific trait: the need to *be* men, *generically*: Pass a guy on the road, and it's guaranteed: a hundred yards on he'll be way ahead again.

A manly woman is much less bent out of gender-shape than a feminine man (as distinct from the best kind, a man who's part woman*). Women practice a different sort of one-upmanship: Intimate a criticism to a young woman. Where a boy will be wounded in his male pride, she'll be offended in her female sensibility and seek relief in an enjoyable bout of passive aggression. So boys are more vulnerable? Yes.

But it's all less true than it was a couple of generations ago—more's the pity. Fixed types, stereotypes, are the delight of people-watchers because they are both impersonally amusing *and* humanly poignant. Why? Because these incarnate schemata were walking incubators of interior individualism, much more so than are the free-form originals who express themselves.

* My personal vocabulary; there's more: Every woman is female, but only some are feminine. "Woman" is an honorific,

"feminine" an ascription varying with taste, "female" (except used biologically) insult-flavored.

Why does talent so often prevent depth? Because if you expend yourself in what you're easily good at, you're tempted not to stop and think.

Shameful reason for writing no more books: not being read. Fair reason for not being read: being unreadable.

There is a special kind of esteem induced by my books, a little deflating but pleasant nonetheless: Friends admire them not because *they've read* them, but because *I wrote* them.

Sunt lacrimae rerum. "Tears there are for things"*— the whole sad and sorry caboodle. Also snickers, for these tear-drawing *res* happen over and over with mechanical regularity, and that's one definition of deflationary comedy.

*Virgil, *Aeneid*.

Words are inadequate—a common, and slightly lazy, wisdom—because they rub out detail and dull down specificity. Keep in mind, however, that thereby they also buffer their rough and rugose object and give it a high finish: the gloss of generality overlaying the grain of particularity.

Mutual opacity: Concerning inmost matters the very exigencies of telling occlude the tale; we become constrictedly inarticulate. "Utterance," outing ourselves (literally), is impeded by urgency. The too-easy claim that people are self-deceived, quasi-innocent liars is probably mostly beside the point. They *would*, if only they adequately *could*, tell true.

Not factual accuracy or rational validity is the required "getting it right" in meditative writing (of course not!), but drawing together salient insights and nailing details, so that, like sinkers on fishing lines, insights will float beneath the surface but above the bottom—that region in which essayistic thought disports itself: between Appearance and Being, where little fishy wisdoms strike and take the hook. (There's nothing like the mess of fresh-caught small fry dipped in beer batter and deep-fried that a guy showed me how to fix—my fish, his beer—on Drummond Island, Michigan.)

This is not hyperbole: the bane of human life is inexpressiveness. In ordinary life, the language-deprived are insipid; in a jam, violent; in desperation, gagged; in love, vapid; in admiration, just inadequate—current example: "very special," as the all-purpose specifier.

Why do people pack their thought in verbal sawdust? Well, perhaps they think that external bulk adds mentational gravitas. But meaning is not amenable to bulking up. Better to blow off the dust, expose the small, but, we hope,* scintillating point.

* *Nota bene: not* "hopefully."

When the depths swim up, they first, perforce, become superficies—then aphorisms, which are skimmed profundities.

Becoming known to people whom you don't know is the initial inhumanity, and let no writers of published books claim they didn't collude. To talk to an addressee who can't respond is eerie; moreover, the thought turns you into an untethered hot air balloon. As my old Russian colleague used to say on the occasion of such realizations: "Discovers America."

But here I am, proclaiming new-old discoveries. Actually, I read it early on in Plato's *Phaedrus*, on the dangers of inhumanly propagated thinking—*writing*. Belatedly, I *did* discover this America, in my own time and by myself: The danger is in "apodictic" writing, in which the author asserts necessary truths in a declarative mode and absconds. So I devised a tentative mood: boldly putting forth and cautiously withdrawing.

Candid review, suppressed: "I would that this book, which has just now appeared, might just as soon disappear." My uncle, music reviewer for the *Vossische Zeitung* between the World Wars: "Last night Herr M. performed Beethoven's Violin Concerto in D. Why?" Keep a mental file of those humanely suppressed witticisms to turn in at Heaven's ticket booth.

A talent for quick conjoining, verbal adequacy, is surely needed for thoughtful living and producing; but submissive receptivity and ready delight trump all that, for these are not supervenient gifts but basic ways of being.

Chatting with my translation buddies about a gay, very masculine-featured poet,* I observe that he must have made many women unhappy: "Not to be wanted in particular is bad, but by reason of one's sex, worse." Peter: "Write that down for your next book. Or perhaps you already have." I hadn't but now I have, though I don't know if Paul will want it.

*Thom Gunn. It was Paul who gave me *On the Move*, Oliver Sacks' autobiography, named after the title of one of Gunn's poems. Sacks gave me a line in *An Anthropologist from Mars* (1995): "Eva Brann, the philosopher, . . ." Naturally I kept the book on my bedside table, and awoke one 3:30 AM to find that it harbored an eery luminous ghost: the jacket glowed! (2016: still does). Refrained from inferences.

Again: the idea that *can* be borrowed deserves to be stolen—it's an idea-item, not a living thought. All learning is permitted plagiarism: You remember a teacher or a writing gratefully and forget what, in particular, you received, because it has become a no longer discernible part of you. To rephrase: only inherently filchable ideas are subject to plagiarism and so punishable.

Here's a contradicting addendum: Written thought, thinking stably sensualized, being now a thing, can be *ipso facto* purloined and is, hence, plagiarized *impermissibly*—because it *is* a thing and things are constitutionally stealable, and stealing is against the Eighth Commandment.

"I took a look at your piece": Meant to win brownie points for the intention, deserving of the author's undying hatred. It's the language of endemic unmeaning, but unlike the check-out counter girl's "Have a nice day," which greases the wheels of civic intercourse, it's grating. After all, you're dealing with the coagulated flow of someone's mind, so the reader's and colleague's eleventh commandment should apply: Thou shalt treat works of the soul with respect. That may mean: critically—severely but seriously. No taking vagrant looks!

What a delightful experience: reading around in a book I wrote and finding it fascinating. Good judgment or terminal narcissism?

Writing a book is being gripped by a continuous possession, and seeing its first copy is undergoing a sudden exorcism.

I love American English in every register: dated slang and with-it lingo, niche-jargon and techno-talk, high-flown rant and prose-poetry—a dedicated diction for every walk of life and motion of the soul.

40 YOUTH

People approve of the young striving to find themselves. Not me: they should lose themselves—in something. Forget identity, espouse alterity, and before you know it, you're yourself.

Young smart-alecks have a vexatious charm—charm because they're smart, vexatious because smart-aleckiness is a cul-de-sac.

Babies (and that rare grown-up) are good company even when asleep.

Teacher seeks to convey evolutionary continuities. Students manage to hear anecdotal high points.

They say: Consorting with the young keeps you young. Not so; at eighty-seven I'm younger than some of my eighteen-year-olds. They know things in their bones (not a good venue for illumination) that I learned recently and reluctantly. They're not very innocent and not really knowledgeable; I'm—well, let that be. But why do I say "They"? Back to "Some."

"They" keep saying that the old stay young by consorting with the young. Ha! The old learn what old is by consorting with the young (both ways: by contrast *and* because the young are pretty sclerotic, sometimes).

The occasional formality of some of our terminally casual kids is simply moving: a consciousness honing the skill of evincing its dignity.

When the sweet-sad nostalgia for what never was infects the intellect, we get idealism, that ornament of young souls and liability for mature actors. "Ornament for the young," because dream-suffused intellecting suits them; "liability for adults," because idealistic mentation unsuitably overbears practicality.

Un-brought-up brats, American kids, wallow in the permissive muck their narrow, driven elders have prepared for them. My bet's on them in a pinch—over the strained virtue of well-brought-up, deliberately deprived paragons from the disciplined households of another age. Even severely inclined parents nowadays are eventually reduced to impotent carping, as their kids are absorbed into the strenuous self-indulgences of teenage culture. And behold: they're quite good to each other—on the whole.

"I know thee not, old man."* I've no affection for fat, smelly, base Falstaff and his lusts for life, but I think young Harry's words are not just gratuitously cruel but wrong-headed (as reasons of state, callow or mature, often are). Maxim: Don't outgrow the friends of your youth, for that's outgrowing yourself, leaving yourself behind when you should keep yourself together, now all present or recallable.

Henry IV.

Just because someone now says what you said earlier, it's not plagiarism, is it? Maybe the subject itself said to him what it said to you. Anyhow, my old rule holds: whoever is the younger at the time when he thought it— he's the one who originated it. The notion of purloining thought only goes for shameless copying but never for that all-unconscious absorption connecting an eager learner to a trusted teacher: That's an honor, although bestowed unconsciously—no, not "although," but *because* so bestowed.

From two to twelve, male sensibility is poignant: awkward grace, conflicted pride, bashful aggression. And always the question: Has the boy's body, with its incipiently erect appendage, informed the soul or did the male soul inform the body even pre-genitally? (If you doubt that soul and body are disparate, get to know a transgendering youngster.)

Can any candid person profess to be a grown-up? One may be a *Respektsperson* (as the Germans say) out in that cut-out of life called the adult world, but surely back at home sprite-like juvenility prevails. Isn't it the mode proper to the life of learning? Come to think of it, can a terminal adult have inner dignity, the kind that emerges when playfulness goes grave?

The example of children: the more sure they are of available comfort the less they need it. So also, mostly, for grown-ups. The unassuageable need of the basically deprived is the devil to deal with, not least because of the harshest of facts: neediness is unattractive, whereas the natural "care-soliciting" (in ethnologic jargon) of young animals is appealing; they're said to have evolved to be cute. (How'd they survive before that?)

Really sad: Someone is trying to cause grief and succeeding only in causing irritation. Queasy-making in adults but heart-rending in children: naughtiness unable to elicit signs of care.

A guarded youth is icky, a candid adult scary.

Boys (up to the age of fifty-five) are vulnerable in their brittle manliness, easily wounded in their pride. Women are offended instead, and this confirms their femininity; they writhe publicly but do not break. Of course, these generalizations are semi-nonsense; there are proud women and aggrieved men.

The adolescent dilemma: Aren't we all always selfish, whether we behave well because it pleases us or behave well because it pleases us to do what doesn't please us? It's true, of course, but by a tautology. Whatever a self does is self-ish—even friendship: alter *ego*. It's possible that "our" post-mortem being will be cosmically diffused, say reunited with the Intellect or the Design of the cosmos, but then we won't be un-selfish but self-less. So the question is: Can we, insuperably self-bound, circumvent the imputation of moral defect that some obsessive young are burdened by? Two answers: 1. No, we're always aboriginally wrong, congenitally afflicted with that *original sin*, our selfhood; don't trust anyone who hasn't ever felt that. 2. Yes, for while you can't shake off constitutional selfishness, you can monitor the nature of your moral *pleasure*: Is it sound, roused by some objective goodness? Then be at peace; your self is saved.

Once again: the young. This is, as I see it, the impending danger to them: their imaginations are so scoured by the acid rain of man-made, utility-loaded pictures that the capacity for the home-made, self-owned, merely imaginative kind is in danger of being obliterated—to wit, the "selfie," whose transmissible antics must surely blot out the self-revealing self-imaging of introspection. Similarly, the enormities, speed- and quantity-wise, of cyberspace experiences can really overwhelm the appetite for reality. (National Park attendance is way down, since, so it is reported, people have seen it all on screens.) Never forget: "cyber" is a masking abbreviation of *kybernan*, related to "govern," to "direct, steer." Electronic space is *superficially* the venue for our whims, but it is *deeply* directive, jigged by interests; it is the reserve of others' purpose—not ours.

There's an eager blather about the openness and flexibility of the young. Not in my experience: They're often indeterminate and unfinished. What else would they be? So they hold on to such fixities as they have, opinionated and recalcitrant. What else would they do? But when an interest takes over, these entrenchments are bypassed and they do lovely learning.

One difference between youth and maturity: You can get more out of the young than they know is in them. Later on you can't get more than there's there, and that will have to do.

It's a pleasing delusion that the young are flexible and receptive; in fact they can be rigid and resistant as hell. These are not age-based features; after all, there's mellowing.

Those deprived kids who belong to the third generation after the sexual revolution are, or so it seems, less experienced in love as a complex passion than as an appetitive project. And no wonder; when society wants to be so encouraging, you need a strong gift for recalcitrant bootstrapping to recover the ardors of non-therapeutic intimacy.

The Germans have a word, *Anschmiegsamkeit*, "the property of snuggling clinglingly up to someone." Why is it so eerie in little children? (Experience from my year-and-a-half as a kindergarten helper.) It's because one suspects some warping of their young souls by a bad situation. Here's what's awful: Ethnologists speak of the care-soliciting behavior of the babies of species, which is designed by nature to elicit a fond response. In short: babies are cute. But a clinging need is not naturally inviting; you have to make yourself respond. It's a vicious circle because the child divines it; a curse on cold parents. But then: Are there naturally unassuagably needy, indefeasibly unattractive kids, pitiable versions of the notorious "bad seed"? However, here's a happy counter-tale: Gabe, a terminally weepy kid, used to climb on my lap to cry the moment his mother shoved him in the door. He did it for two weeks or so, then looked up at the room full of toys, jumped down, and thereafter would hardly give me the time of day. And his mother was grateful to boot.

There are people who, being past (or never up to) derring-do, insouciantly urge the young into the jaws of death—repulsive surrogate-seekers. Why don't young jihadists ever seem to say to their pious handlers: "What about you go?" (There is an answer, actually: the terrible notion that heaven can be gained by sending others.)

The paradox of caring love (with a view to half-grown children): What's on offer is love, what's wanted is liberty. Love is to bow out, to accomplish the inherently impossible: self-removal. So progenitors must live a paradox: to give by not giving. Brutally put: Pay the tuition, hold the closeness, "absent thee from felicity *awhile*." As a fellow adult, I feel for the parents; as a teacher, I'm with the fledgling kids.

A serious boy is one of the wonders of the world. We have few girls; they mostly come as women.

Are feminine women ever young, really young, like young men?

Advice to the psycho-managers: tell the kids to lower their self-esteem and raise their self-respect.

Why the young are often shy but more rarely reticent: because beneath their inhibitions they know that self-disclosure is a legitimate part of their becoming, their coming-out.

For the young, inhibited and impetuous, talking about themselves is a risky and pleasant activity, like a somewhat dangerous sport which makes them feel at once their own ponderous gravity and light-footed facility. They're giving something away and they're imposing something on you, under conditions of sloppy practice and insufficient language. You're now co-owner of their inward life, expected to particularize the formulaically inadequate speech employed by them for self-revelation. And slick or halting, they're usually language-challenged in intimate communication, which requires an artfulness that comes with maturity. So they're simultaneously boring and charming. The tedium makes listening a duty, the charm makes it a welcome one.

In some adults, it's more rehearsed—a canned autobiography, prepared for the broad pleasure of self-diffusion (with a tinge of remaindered shame). In others, it's heart-rending, and everything in you goes on alert: Can I summon the required judgment-informed sympathy?

The bane of the young: their near and dear who want to be told but don't want to hear.

Little boys are those fallen angels that, being too small and too light to tumble the length of the whole cosmos, landed on earth; they evince Satan's pride and his taste for trouble. I learned this working in the kindergarten. Once with us, their lot is to become respectable men.

EPILOGUE*

To stop is not to end,
To leave off not to finish.
There's much I might amend,
And some t'would not diminish
    The whole, to mark " ℘."

Yet "*stet*," and let them be,
These thoughtlets I have hosted,
Meaning, it's not just me:
Now and again I've ghosted
    For truths I chanced to meet.

* For non-publishing readers: ℘ is a copyeditor's mark for
"delete," *stet* for "let it stand."

Eva Brann was born in Berlin in 1929 into a Jewish family. In 1941 she came to Brooklyn as a refugee from the Nazis. She went to Brooklyn College, then to Yale University, where she studied Classics and Ancient History. She was a member of the American School of Classical Studies at Athens and of its excavations of the Athenian Agora (Marketplace), charged with publishing some of its early pottery.* In 1957 she joined the faculty of St. John's College, Annapolis, and later Santa Fe, in whose all-required Great Books program she has taught ever since, except for 1990–1997, when she was dean of its eastern campus.

* *Potsherds* might, in fact, have been an apt title for this collection: found fragments, parts of an entirety buried too deep for human digging.